Second Language Learning through Drama

Drama is increasingly being recognised as a valuable pedagogy for language learning as it can harness children's imaginations and stimulate their desire to communicate. *Second Language Learning through Drama* draws on current theories of additional and foreign language learning and illustrates through practical case studies how drama can be used to support the four key skills of listening, speaking, reading and writing.

Drawing on the work of an international group of practitioners who are all highly experienced in using drama for the purpose of second language learning, the book clearly explains key drama conventions and strategies and outlines the innovative ways in which they have been used to create enjoyable and stimulating classroom activities that allow for multiple ways of learning.

Throughout the book the emphasis is on making language learning accessible and relevant to children and young people through creative, physically active and playful approaches. The strategies described are all highly flexible and readily adaptable to different teaching contexts. Specific themes include:

- using stories and drama to motivate learners at all levels;
- drama, language learning and identity;
- assessment opportunities through process drama;
- issues of language learning and cultural empowerment;
- digital storytelling;
- film and drama aesthetics.

Second Language Learning through Drama will be of great interest to those studying on undergraduate and postgraduate courses and will serve as a highly valuable text to practitioners looking to incorporate the approaches described into their lessons and classroom activities.

Joe Winston is Professor of Drama and Arts Education at the University of Warwick. He previously taught French as well as drama at primary and secondary level. His previous publications include *Beginning Drama 4–11* (with Miles Tandy, Fulton, 2008), *Drama and English at the Heart of the Primary Curriculum* (Fulton, 2004) and *Drama, Literacy and Moral Education* (Fulton, 2000).

Second Language Learning through Drama

Practical techniques and applications

Edited by
Joe Winston

Routledge
Taylor & Francis Group

LONDON AND NEW YORK

First published 2012
by Routledge
2 Park Square, Milton Park, Abingdon, Oxon OX14 4RN

Simultaneously published in the USA and Canada
by Routledge
711 Third Avenue, New York, NY 10017

Routledge is an imprint of the Taylor & Francis Group, an informa business

British Library Cataloguing in Publication Data
A catalogue record for this book is available from the British Library

Library of Congress Cataloging in Publication Data
Second language learning through drama: practical techniques and
applications / edited by Joe Winston.—1st ed.
     p. cm.
1. Language and languages—Study and teaching. 2. Second language
acquisition—Study and teaching. 3. Drama in education. I. Winston,
Joe, 1953– II. Title.
P53.297.S43 2011
418.0071—dc22   2011007878

ISBN: 978–0–415–59778–4 (hbk)
ISBN: 978–0–415–59779–1 (pbk)
ISBN: 978–0–203–80511–4 (ebk)

Typeset in Bembo
by Book Now Ltd, London

MIX
Paper from
responsible sources
FSC
www.fsc.org   FSC® C004839

Printed and bound in Great Britain by
TJ International Ltd, Padstow, Cornwall

Contents

Illustrations

Contributors

Li-Yu Sabina Chang completed her PhD at the University of Warwick, UK, and is currently Assistant Professor in the Department of Drama Creation and Application at National University of Tainan, Taiwan. As teacher, trainer and writer, she takes a keen interest in bringing drama, story and language teaching together to develop effective methods catering for young learners.

Astrid Yi Mei Chung taught English in senior high schools in Taiwan for seven years before she embarked upon her PhD research at the University of Warwick, UK. Her research interests include drama pedagogy and how these approaches resonate with current second language teaching and learning theories.

Deborah Hull is the Artistic and Educational Director of The Play House, a theatre education charity based in Birmingham, UK. She has an MA in Drama and Theatre Education from the University of Warwick and has co-authored a chapter in the 2007 IDEA World Congress Handbook.

Tanya Kempston is a Teaching Consultant in the University of Hong Kong. Prior to this, she was a Curriculum Development Officer in the Hong Kong Education Bureau and worked as an ESL teacher in Hong Kong and Japan for several years.

Kirsty McGeoch has worked as an English language teacher for 14 years in Australia and in other countries. She is in the final stages of completing her PhD thesis on digital storytelling in second language learning through the University of Sydney.

Erene Palechorou works as a full-time teacher in Cypriot primary schools and is currently completing her PhD thesis with the University of Warwick, UK. Her research focus is on how drama, as a pedagogic method, can facilitate the acquisition of Greek as an additional language by ethnic minority children in Cypriot primary schools.

Erika C. Piazzoli teaches Italian and drama at Griffith University in Brisbane, Australia. She is also completing a PhD in the aesthetics of process drama for teaching Additional Languages. Erika's recent publications can be found in *Research in Drama Education* (vol. 15, no. 3) and *IDEA* (vol. 11).

Julia Rothwell spent six years lecturing in Languages Curriculum at Queensland University of Technology, Australia, and is an experienced language teacher at primary and middle school level. Her doctoral thesis explores the connections between process drama and the intercultural literacy of beginner language learners.

Madonna Stinson is Senior Lecturer at Griffith University, Australia. Her interests lie in drama curriculum, language acquisition and curriculum design and implementation. Her most recent book (co-authored with John O'Toole and Tiina Moore) is *Drama and Curriculum: A giant at the door.*

Joe Winston is Professor of Drama and Arts Education at the University of Warwick and is co-editor of *Research in Drama Education*. He is well known internationally for his publications and for his teaching. His latest book, *Beauty and Education*, was published by Routledge in 2010.

Burcu Yaman Ntelioglou is a doctoral candidate at the Ontario Institute for Studies in Education, University of Toronto specialising in second/additional language education and drama and curriculum studies. Her publications include *Crossing Borders: Drama in the Second Language Classroom* (2007).

Acknowledgements

With special thanks to BekaFilms, Melo Prino and Domenico Lannutti for providing the film stills from '*Buongiorno*' (Chapter 11).

Introduction

Second and Additional Language Learning through Drama

Joe Winston

I began my teaching career in the late 1970s not as a drama specialist but as a teacher of modern languages, principally French, in a comprehensive school in the north of England. I was fortunate to be in a modern, well-equipped department with its own specialist facilities and a suite of three rooms, one of which was a fully functioning language laboratory with individual carrels and up to date tape decks. Audio visual screens and strong sound systems were permanent fixtures in each of the other rooms, all of which carried colourful and attractive displays. This was all very different from my own, grammar school education, which had centred around a series of grammar based textbooks authored by a man our French teacher referred to as 'Willie Whitmarsh', written on the assumption that French was something you learned principally in order to read the classics of its literature and understand the nuances of its grammar. We had been taught nothing about the everyday culture of France – about croissants, baguettes, yellow post boxes and 2CV cars which I had discovered somewhat bewilderingly on my first trip to France at the age of 18. Nor had we been taught to speak it very much. This was far removed from the modernity of the new, vibrant modern languages department in which I now taught. The new textbooks had pictures and emphasised everyday vocabulary and everyday life in France. The principal mode of pedagogy was through audio visual resources, with phrases to repeat and use. Oral competence was deemed central and *a priori* to reading and writing.

Despite all of this, large numbers of students remained stubbornly disinterested in French. France was far away, the majority did not hanker after visiting it and seemed to have little motivation to learn its language. And the flash, new resources could not mask the shortcomings of the textbooks which the vast majority of the students found off-putting. After all, who wants to learn about a boring family in a series of boring pictures who go about leading deeply boring lives and having tedious conversations, mainly in

1

the present tense? There were, in other words, major flaws in the pedagogical model promoted by the textbooks, despite their multimodal nature.

Of course, if I were to enter a modern language classroom in a school nowadays I would expect to find that things have changed, and would surely be impressed by the vastly superior and sophisticated possibilities afforded by modern technologies, and their ability to bring the target culture graphically and phonically into the classroom in an instant and to make face to face communication with speakers of the language so much easier. Yet, once again, the problem of interest, of motivation has not been automatically solved by new technologies and newly designed curricula; within the UK and other Anglophonic countries, take-up of modern languages for advanced study in state schools continues to decline.

Globalisation may be partly responsible for this. For better or for worse, English has become a dominant world language and the social and economic necessity to speak another language is less marked for those young people who have English as their mother tongue. We might expect motivation to learn English to be far greater in a country such as China, where recent educational reforms have emphasised its central importance for the future citizens of the country,[1] or in Taiwan, where many children are sent by their parents to learn it after normal school hours in private language schools. As is made clear in Chapters 3 and 8, however, the preferences of parents will not necessarily increase young people's interest, motivation or levels of performance if the pedagogy remains stubbornly traditional and rooted in textbook learning. Young people the world over will not find interest in English simply because they are told that learning it will help them in some future career.

Globalisation has brought another, more complex challenge to the learning and teaching of languages in schools. If many of the students I taught remained stubbornly monolingual, it did not create challenges for teachers of other subjects. With the dramatic increases in immigration experienced by developed countries in recent years, however, the presence of a multitude of additional languages has become more and more common in classrooms in all phases of schooling. As a result, teaching students in a language other than their mother tongue is no longer the preserve of modern language teachers and the need to find pedagogies to address this challenge successfully is increasingly pressing.

This book is intended as a practical resource for all who have an interest in developing effective pedagogies to support second and additional language learning. The chapters are written by a range of experienced teachers and researchers who work across four continents – Australasia, Asia, Europe and North America. They speak a range of mother tongues – English, Greek, Italian, Mandarin Chinese and Turkish – and the target languages they teach include English, German, Greek and Italian. What they share is a belief that drama can be a particularly effective means to address some of the challenges of teaching additional and second languages in both primary and secondary classrooms across the globe. They share, too, a common understanding of drama, sometimes referred to as 'process drama': drama not as the rehearsal and performance of plays but as an interactive, participatory form of pedagogy that engages learners emotionally and playfully and that has an established tradition of practices that are growing in their international impact.

The chapters present examples of successful projects at all levels of schooling, from early years to upper secondary. Some are case studies of teachers using drama to help teach children an additional language, others are based firmly in the second or 'foreign' language classroom. Although they concentrate on practice, certain common theoretical themes underpin this practice, either implicitly or explicitly, and their articulation will help explain why drama pedagogies can make a significant contribution to students' second and additional language learning.

Throughout this book, language learning is not understood as a simple, technical process – the learning of a set of skills, words and phrases – but as deeply cultural in its nature. A language different from my mother tongue presents me with a contrasting way of perceiving and understanding my place in the world by confronting me with the reality of how others understand and communicate that world.[2] As the key means by which a culture expresses its values, conventions and rules, it is part of a wider network of meanings which also find living expression in customs, beliefs, traditions, cooking, songs, rituals and, in particular, the stories a people tell themselves about themselves. None of these are fixed and monolithic, however, particularly in today's globalised world. Cultures and languages are porous; they meet, interact, exchange and slowly transform as they mutually influence one another. Nevertheless, in an education system, one language and culture – or 'languaculture' as it has been termed by Agar (1996) – is likely to be dominant and powerful, and for children being educated entirely in a language different from their mother tongue, their very sense of identity can be at stake, their self esteem and self confidence at risk, factors which are bound to have a strong impact on their education as a whole. In the case studies presented in Chapters 3, 4, 7 and 10, we see explicitly how drama projects have helped address these very issues in different ways, in different contexts and for students of different ages.

One key way in which drama manages this is by encouraging students to experiment safely with alternative identities and hence come to see and imagine themselves differently, and the benefits of this extend to second as well as additional language learners. This loosening of what I have previously called the 'tyranny of identity' (Winston, 2004, p. 12) can alter students' sense of self, heighten their perceived status in the classroom and thus encourage them to find a voice. The roles they play, if engaging enough, can serve the same, liberating function of a mask, enabling them to feel safe enough to take risks with language that they would otherwise feel too self conscious to attempt.

Such work can also open up what has been called an 'affective space', a psychic space in which students become engaged emotionally with the thrill, tension or straightforward enjoyment of a developing story. This level of engagement is far removed from the miniature role plays that are common in second language classrooms, in which, for example, I pretend to be a waiter and you pretend to order a drink from me. Such simple exercises have their place, for sure, but they are entirely cognitive in their aims, and thus run the risk of becoming repetitive, predictable and boring. If we can manage to make students feel emotionally energised in the service of the target language, once again, they are far more likely to try to use the language and dig deeply into the linguistic resources they possess in order to communicate through it. If I am using the target language to try and find a missing girl (Chapter 4), to bargain with a ship's captain for more food and water (Chapter 5), or to argue my innocence of a crime I have been accused of (Chapter 8), the stakes will feel notably higher, provided I have been successfully lured into playing the fictional game that the teacher has set up.

Drama projects, then, when planned well, can bring the feeling of authenticity to the communication process because they provide contexts for language that are dynamic and that feel real. The concepts of 'authentic tasks' and 'authentic learning' are not unknown in second language classrooms. Take cookery, for example: following a recipe and instructions in another language and only being allowed to communicate in that language is one way to use the target language purposefully to produce something of value. Authentic tasks can also help students make use of different linguistic registers, the more formal setting of an interview, for example, or the language that typifies an advertisement. In drama the authenticity is imagined, and hence the possible range of such tasks is expansive, but they must be willingly entered into on the part of the students. This not only means that teachers need to be skilful in how they match projects to the interests of learners but also that they must be prepared to be playful, appreciative of the energising potential of play as something far removed from mere frivolity. The playful spirit of drama is what makes it enjoyable and this enjoyment can lure students into becoming more receptive to the target language and more willing to make use of it. This play can readily extend to the musical qualities of the language itself, to the sounds and rhythms of words and phrases, the kind of play exemplified for young learners in some of the activities described in Chapters 2 and 3 and for advanced learners in Chapter 9, in which a class of Taiwanese students are introduced to the language of Shakespeare.

One of the key advantages that drama pedagogy can bring to the language classroom is its recognition of the centrality of the body in the learning process. Classrooms on the whole are still places founded on the Cartesian idea that the brain and the body are two distinct entities; that the brain is the site of learning and that the body gets in the way of this by being prone to fidgeting, doodling, getting tired and wanting to go to the toilet. Drama, on the other hand, seeks to channel and liberate the body's energies through playful, physical activity and – particularly significant for additional and second language learning – it foregrounds the communicative potential of bodies through their uses of non verbal or 'paralinguistic' signs. Gestures, facial expressions, body language – how I sit, where I stand in relation to other people, whether I have my back turned or not, whether I am crouched in a corner or standing boldly in the centre of a space – all of these communicate meaning. They are ways in which students can make human sense of communicative acts, ways they can readily deploy themselves in order to support their use of words. Many gestures and facial expressions are cross cultural and easy to use and recognise; but the more culturally specific – how the French tap the left hand twice under the right hand to signify 'let's go!', for example – can be learned and played with, serving not only to embody my relationship with the target language but also, crucially, with the people who use it.

Because it makes use of the body in this way, drama is essentially a multimodal form of pedagogy, offering different points of entry for students' interests to be engaged. Good language teachers already make use of visual aids, of animation, of sound, of the possibilities afforded by new technologies. Drama, too, offers visual and auditory signs for students to make sense of but the difference is that the multimodality of drama pedagogy largely depends upon the presence of live bodies; it is interactive, immediate and able to respond and adapt swiftly to student comments, questions and ideas. A teacher in role is able to vary her or his vocabulary, repeat and simplify her or his questions, feign misunderstanding, sigh in disbelief, show excitement or hurt. She or he is able, in other words, to improvise and make a range of multimodal responses in order to encourage, develop, re-enforce, support or extend students' use of the target language in much more direct, flexible and human ways than even the most advanced piece of technology. And a visual 'aid' in drama, such as a book or a diary, is more than a cue to repeat 'voici un livre' or to put up your hand and say 'c'est un carnet'. It will have symbolic significance, be important to the development of a plot, offer the promise of information that could tell us something important about a character; in other words, visuals are far more engaging, more powerfully communicative, when used well in drama.

Finally, one of the potential strengths of drama for language teachers is its social nature. Students being able and willing to work together, watch and listen to one another, talk through ideas and improvise together, shape material and present it in groups – such is the very stuff of the drama classroom. The spirit that characterises such work at its best is that of the ensemble – where everyone supports everyone else for the benefit of the whole group. Such an atmosphere is necessarily founded on trust and co-operation and will, when achieved, encourage students to find their own voices, lose their inhibitions, contribute and speak out in class.

These substantial advantages do not come automatically, however. The book does not offer drama as a panacea, as a magic formula, as something readily packaged and easy to deliver with a minimum amount of thought and effort on the part of the teacher. Even the most experienced of drama teachers will often need to be patient, reflective, flexible and willing to re-think and adapt their plans in response to the students they are working with. Nor is the book claiming that drama should be regarded as *the* language pedagogy *per se*. Of course it shouldn't. Nevertheless, the chapters that follow outline approaches and detail projects that make clear how teachers, internationally and across the age ranges, can and do make use of drama to support second and additional language learning and the extent to which their achievements can be assessed, evaluated and found to be highly effective.

Notes

1   See Xiaohong and Zeegers (2010)
2   For a particularly vivid example of this see Kaplan (1993).

References

Agar, M. (1996) *Language Shock: Understanding the Culture of Conversation.* New York: Quill, William Morrow.

Kaplan, A. (1993) *French Lessons: A memoir.* Chicago: University of Chicago Press.

Winston, J. (2004) *Drama and English at the Heart of the Curriculum.* London: David Fulton.

Xiaohong, Zhang and Zeegers, M. (2010) Redefining the Role of English as a Foreign Language in the Curriculum in the Global Context. *Changing English, 17*(2), 177–187.

1

'Dramatic' Language Learning in the Classroom

Li-Yu Sabina Chang

The introduction has briefly sketched some of the theoretical foundations that underpin the practice outlined in the following chapters. This chapter, while echoing some of the points made in the introduction, points to additional theoretical and research evidence to argue for the effectiveness of drama pedagogy specifically in the area of second language learning. In doing so, I make reference throughout to some of the common strategies or conventions that drama teachers make use of to structure their lessons. A glossary of these terms can be found at the end of this book for the benefit of non-drama specialists.

Learning through drama

Drama is unique in its creative and symbolic use of space, time and human presence. In drama, time can be altered, space changed and identities shifted. By means of drama conventions, an imagined context can be created in which the class and teacher are able to suspend their disbelief "in order to pretend, as a group, that they are *other* people, in *another* place, in *another* time" (Neelands, 1984, p. 46). The transformations of space, time and identities make it possible for students to "try out and experiment with new ideas, concepts, values, roles and language in action" as Neelands (1984, p. 6) suggests. In addition, they can put themselves in others' shoes and make decisions in a non-threatening dramatic world without worrying about the unpleasant consequences their actions in real life might bring to them. Participating in drama activities can help develop children's personal resources such as self-confidence, self-esteem, social skills, communication, emotional resilience, empathy, physical expressiveness, collaborative and cooperative skills and processes (Pascoe et al., 2004, p. 122). As I shall now go on to argue, most of these benefits of drama pedagogy coincide with key factors that contribute to children's learning in general and to second language acquisition in particular.

Multiple ways of learning

Drama, as a multimodal art form combining visual, aural, verbal and kinaesthetic languages, offers students "different points of entry into the work and different ways of becoming involved" (Nicholson, 2000, p. 179). Engaging in multiple ways of learning enables children to fix the learning experience more firmly in their minds. For instance, those children who respond particularly well to visual stimuli or who have good spatial awareness will benefit from drama activities such as creating still images and sculpting partners. These can also be enjoyed kinaesthetically, by children who like to touch, move around and manipulate objects. Miming and acting out may well attract them into taking part. Drama conventions such as voices in the head, conscience alley, hot seating and sound collage have an auditory appeal for those who are good at verbal exchanges and mimicking sounds. From these examples, we can see that drama can stimulate the visual, kinaesthetic and auditory aspects of learning and therefore allow more children to feel confident as learners as a variety of "points of entry" are being addressed.

Drama and oracy

Talking helps us clarify our thoughts and understand our feelings. As an old saying goes, "How can I know what I think, until I hear what I say?" Kempe and Holroyd (2004, p. 5) make it clear that "It is through the act of articulating ideas that those ideas become crystallised." Drama is a collectively constructed, imagined world that demands a positive and supportive working atmosphere. Students need to take part in group discussions and, as a result, can learn and gain support from their peers. Moreover, the playful nature of drama is conducive to preparing learners to articulate their thoughts and take risks. However, second language teachers will often complain about the difficulty of getting students to respond in class. Some will fill the silence with their own talk because the students' non-participation in classroom activities and discussion unnerves them. So what is it that makes students feel inhibited when it comes to speaking in the language class-room? A brief statement from The British Council-Hornby Seminars in English Language Teaching (2006) provides one sensible answer: "Students often do not have a real reason to speak because the tasks do not motivate them or do not require them to say anything which they find meaningful." If this is the case, it is insufficient for teachers to provide pupils with superficial contexts designed only for practising language skills. Byron (1986) draws a fine line between the real demands of language use and the time spent by learners overtly practising "skills" targeted at but distant from a time when they might need these skills for real. Emphasising the importance of the demands of the "as if" situation instead of the language skills, he explains:

> as human beings, we have a marked propensity to become absorbed in an "as if" world, so that it begins to *feel real*: not real in the sense that it is actually happening, but real in the sense that the problems faced and the outcomes *matter* to the participant.
>
> (p. 126)

To break students' silence, then, teachers need to engage them emotionally; and within the context of drama, this means that teachers must make the dramatic situation *matter* to their students. The success of language development through drama depends on whether students "care enough about the problem in the drama to try and meet the challenges (including the language challenge) it offers" (Byron, 1986, p. 127).

Role-taking and role-creating in educational drama give students a chance to put themselves in others' shoes in an imagined context. Not only does the pretending bring about an immediate need for students to communicate, it also has the potential to change the power structure and interaction patterns in the classroom. Take teacher-in-role for example. When taking a role, the teacher needs to go beyond the functions he/she usually performs as "an instructor, model and resource" (Kao & O'Neill, 1998, p. 2) so that students can use language creatively and respond appropriately to how the teacher behaves and speaks in role. O'Toole (2008) suggests a number of roles, both in high- or low-status positions, which teachers can play in order to put pressure on students' language output. His suggestions include being someone who has information but is reluctant or unable to deliver it coherently; someone who is in need of information or help; someone who drops a bombshell but takes no responsibility; or someone who is a provocateur (p. 26). This strategy also serves to draw the class together, "in listening, thinking, and building the event with speculation and anticipation as they look for clues to the emerging dramatic world in which they participate" (Liu, 2002, p. 68).

In drama class, a fictional world is constructed but this can only happen through mutual participation, a fact that can provide students with a sense of ownership and the motivation to contribute verbally in order to keep the drama going and extend its scope and depth. In a well-designed dramatic situation, the learners' need for communication tends to overcome their fear of linguistic inadequacy so that they are able to make the best use of the language skills they already possess (Somers, 1994, p. 139). Drama is a key way to maximise opportunities for pupils' oracy, thus paving the way for developing their literacy.

Drama and literacy

Becoming literate

Definitions of literacy range widely. For some, literacy is simply the ability to read and write various types of text to meet the basic need for communication. For others, being literate has much broader connotations and involves a capacity for manipulating language and utilising modes of discourse for a specific purpose and audience. As Corden (2000) puts it, "literacy is a problematic concept, dependent on a number of factors and what a particular culture or society deems to be important and relevant" (p. 28). How we define literacy will influence how we teach it. So, before exploring how drama can facilitate its development, some of the meanings underlying the term, literacy, need first of all to be untangled.

If being literate is equated with being able to read and write, then literacy teaching will entail the mastery of a set of discrete linguistic skills which enable students to decode meanings from texts as well as produce them. In such an approach, literacy teaching will concentrate on the imparting of knowledge of three cueing systems – graphophonic (letter/ sound relationships), syntactic (grammar and structure of sentences) and semantic (meaning of the text). The danger here, as Winston (2004) has pointed out, is that, if we regard language merely as a body of skills to be mastered and deployed, then we are likely to divorce language exercises from context, "as it is the skill rather than the experience that is seen as important" (p. 20). This is not to reject the importance of skills-based literacy;

Cameron (2001) has argued that "learning the detail of how texts are written and can be understood is crucial to children's educational and personal development" (p. 125). It should not, however, be considered as the one and only all-important aspect in the teaching of literacy. Literacy is about language and the cueing systems are only part of language.

Halliday (1970) has proposed an influential theoretical framework in which language is analysed in terms of four strata: Context, Semantics, Lexico-Grammar and Phonology-Graphology. He maintains that language performs three metafunctions:

- Ideational function: used for the expression of content;

- Interpersonal function: used to maintain and establish social relations;

- Textual function: used to provide cohesive relations within spoken or written texts.

(p. 143)

He goes on to argue that social context, a decisive factor in one's choice of register, includes three situational variables:

- Field: an ongoing social activity or a subject matter of a text;

- Tenor: the relations among the participants;

- Mode: physical medium adopted for communication including the channel and the rhetorical mode.

(Halliday & Hasan, 1985, p. 12)

These three variables which realise context are correspondingly related to the three metafunctions of language. That is, the ideational function is effectuated by means of the field, the interpersonal by means of the tenor and the textual by means of the mode. Halliday's theoretical framework suggests that language is a socially constructed system. Viewing language in a social semiotic way, he suggests that it is essential to bring contexts of situation into focus in order to understand the functions of specific linguistic structures and examine meaning potential. He writes:

We do not experience language in isolation … but always in relation to a scenario, some background of persons and actions and events from which the things which are said derive their meaning. This is referred to as the "situation", so language is said to function in "contexts of situation" and any account of language which fails to build in the situation as an essential ingredient is likely to be artificial and unrewarding.

(Halliday, 1978, pp. 28–29)

According to this view, being literate is a more complex concept which goes far beyond the acquisition of a set of decontextualised coding and decoding skills. It involves the ability to produce and interpret texts in a given context where the realisation of meaning potential deeply depends upon one's social and cultural identity. The importance of contextualisation in language learning has also been stressed by Donaldson. She contends, "the child does not interpret words in isolation – he interprets situation" (Donaldson, 1978, p. 88). On the subject of second language learning, Brown (2001) also strongly advises teachers to take account of contextual considerations in teaching children. As a result, the context of a situation should not be separated from literacy teaching.

Drama as a context for reading

Learning to read is a multifaceted and complicated process. Written texts differ from spoken language, which is normally accompanied by paralinguistic features and interpersonal exchanges that aid the child's comprehension of the utterance. The reader needs to discover and construct the context embedded in the print on the page which is "featureless and does nothing visually to capture the attention or involve the emotions" (Reid, 1991, p. 73). For beginners, according to Reid (1991), "there is loss and change in the transfer to print – loss of immediacy of relevance, loss of vividness, loss of support in the search for meaning" (p. 73). Facing the written text alone, readers will need to rely chiefly on their background knowledge and decoding skills in order to infer meaning from the text.

Young learners of a foreign language need more visual and aural assistance in order to understand a text. Byron (1986) observes that young learners in general are "stronger at reading action, or words–embedded–in–action, than they are at reading words alone" (p. 79). Images, both still and moving, play an influential part in children's perception of meaning. Acknowledging the importance of the visual in young people's lives and the increasing use of multimodal texts in today's technological world, Kress and Van Leeuwen (2006) urge that children's ability to use elements of "visual grammar" should be developed further at school by encouraging them to "actively experiment with the representational resources of word and image, and with the ways in which they can be combined" (p. 113). Drama makes the literary world more accessible for children because it permits them to turn the abstract written words into concrete images and to construct meaning from the text through collective as well as individual experience. Through drama, children can be encouraged to enter a fictional world created by an author, physically taking on roles in order to explore what it is like to be a character in a story. This emotional engagement can motivate them to keep on reading and may well encourage them no longer to see the written text as dull and featureless print on paper but as the entry point into an enjoyable, lively, imaginary world. However, the challenge for teachers here is to find suitable stories that motivate students to explore and use the target language

Skilful writers often leave gaps in the text for readers to fill in. The teacher can use drama activities such as hot seating, thought tracking, interviews, interrogations and gossip circle (Neelands, 2004, pp. 100–105) for children to mine the potential that these gaps present. Where in the story, for example, are there unrecorded conversations, unmentioned thoughts, off-the-page scenarios, possible but undescribed meetings (Grainger, 2004, p. 96)? In exploring these "creative gaps" dramatically, children are able to enter the inner lives of characters and gain "a sense of co-authorship of the text and collaboration with the author" (Baldwin & Fleming, 2003, p. 19). Such experiences can also, as Winston (2004) has pointed out, serve "to stimulate higher order skills of inferring meaning from text, of critically engaging with it and, where appropriate, of expressively articulating it" (p. 26).

Drama as a catalyst for writing

Writing requires a clear Audience, Purpose and Topic, to be "APT" (Cameron, 2001, p. 156), if it is to avoid being reduced to tasks of skill-building aimed solely at mastering the rules of punctuation, spelling, grammar and writing structure. This toolkit approach "will produce competent, though, *disengaged*, writers" (Packwood & Messenheimer, 2003, p. 145). Within a dramatic framework, students take on roles, interact with other characters and enact their situations in order to experience their dilemmas, feel the tension and share in their happiness or sadness. Grainger (2005) argues that this emotional engagement and identification with characters enhances "authenticity and often a real sense of audience" (p. 82). Steele (2003) views working in role as a unique way for learners to think, talk, respond and interact for a change of perspective to occur. She claims that slowing down action by using drama activities such as thought tracking, hot seating and freeze framing, can help students "delve deeper and more reflectively" (p. 184). Through drama, children link together the "there and then" in stories and the world of "here and now", building their understanding upon their experience in drama, which "can bring vividness and an authentic voice" (p. 185) to their writing.

Learners can practise writing in various registers and genres in accordance with the situation of context created in the imaginary world. Let us take an example for second language learners in the primary classroom: the story of *Chicken Licken*. If the children are asked to write in role as the animals telling the King that the sky is falling, they need the words necessary to express their worry and anxiety. They also need to learn how to compose a formal letter including an appropriate greeting, complimentary closure and some suitably polite phrases. In other words, both appropriate vocabulary and an appropriate register should be selected in tune with the status of the characters in the imagined context. This particular, fictional writing demand, a letter to a person in authority, provides a context in which pupils are also required to pay extra attention to spelling, grammar and punctuation. Writing in drama can thus make skills-based language activities more purposeful.

Different drama conventions can act as catalysts for various forms of writing. Grainger (2004, pp. 96–103) suggests a list of drama activities which naturally generate different genres. Freeze frames, for instance, lead to narrative writing; thought tracking supports writing in the reflective mode, such as a diary or letter writing; hot seating can prompt news articles or magazine interviews; formal meetings can be drawn on to draft minutes, official records or posters. Research by Crumpler and Schneider (2002) has shown that discussion methods in a more traditional classroom are less effective in improving children's writing skills. Talk in the drama world, on the contrary, can serve as an oral rehearsal for writing. Composing within a dramatic frame involves "thinking, listening, creating, and doing and engaged learners' repertoire of strategies", and most importantly, gives them the freedom to "use their whole being in meaning-making" (p. 62).

Learning to become literate is not a static process but a dynamic progression of meaning negotiation. Provided that children can fully participate in it, with their bodies as well as their brains, they can maximise their learning potential. Literacy skills should not be viewed narrowly as synonymous with linguistic abilities; it is the context of a situation that should be placed at the heart of literacy curricula, in second language as well as mother tongue learning. A great number of studies (e.g., Cremin, Goouch, Blakemore, Goff, & Macdonald, 2006; Podlozny, 2000; Wagner, 1998) have suggested that learning within the dramatic framework embraces all these important factors in literacy development. Drama can help bring written texts off the page into the here and now and can activate children into listening to one another, having their own say, and trying out a range of registers in order to communicate in context.

Drama and non-verbal communication

Solely interpreting the spoken words of others is insufficient for successful communication as there is a tendency that one's visual and aural signals will carry more messages than one's utterances. These paralinguistic features of communication include facial expressions, gestures and tone of voice. In a traditional second language classroom, very often, teachers cram their students with vocabulary and grammar while the learners remain seated, listening passively. One possible reason for neglecting non-verbal activities may be that they do not seem to generate much language output. Nevertheless, what teachers are in danger of missing is the broader benefit that physical activities can bring to their students. Young learners are physically active by nature and their energies need to be suitably channelled and made use of so that they can concentrate and be responsive in language lessons. Donoghue and Kunkle (1979) explain that active practice, such as acting out commands in the target language, benefits children's language learning in two respects. First, it enhances listening comprehension by activating both the internal semantic systems and psychomotor systems, which improves recall of the second language. Second, it helps to reduce fidgeting in class. Culham (2002) also attests that the incorporation of movement into children's learning experiences can facilitate their recall of a new word, concept or sequence of information.

The physicality of drama caters for children's need to be physically active and, in addition, provides them with opportunities to be fully aware of non-verbal elements of language. Through dramatising a text, as Rastelli (2006) argues, "we give life to the words written on the page and help students become aware of speech features, paralinguistic and extra linguistic features" (p. 82). Drama, to quote Evans (1984), "has the capacity for tuning the ear to the nuances of meaning by encouraging pupils to look behind and beyond the face value of words" (p. 49). In drama activities such as still image or tableau, pupils, either as individuals or as a group, create a frozen image using their own bodies to capture a moment in time, depict a picture or crystallise an idea. It is a highly controlled way to suspend time in drama which gives the participants "pause to gaze and reflect and to inquire into human behaviour" (Winston & Tandy, 2009, p. 34). The open interpretation of body language that freeze frames can encourage can allow students both to express (as a performer) and to articulate (as an observer) the ways in which meaning can be conveyed through subtle changes in non-verbal signals such as expression, gesture and position.

Paralinguistic vocal elements reinforce spoken messages by adding mood, personality and atmosphere. Working in drama, students can incorporate a great many vocal elements to represent characters, create a mood, increase vocal dynamics or respond to different circumstances in the dramatic context. It also encourages clarity of articulation and diction when presenting work to their peers. Unlike the tedious dialogues in many second language textbooks which are normally read out in dull, monotonous voices, the dialogic texts derived from drama and embedded in stories have a better chance of engaging students' emotions and hence enhancing their vocal interpretations. In this way, drama can be one of the most suitable ways to help them to "speak with more confidence, with better articulation and resonance (quality and volume)" and learn how to use voice to "convey different emotions (inflexion, tone/pitch and intonation)" (Almond, 2005, p. 64). In addition, Almond (2005) suggests that learners are able to practise the broader aspects of communication through drama, such as "gesture and gesticulation, facial expression, eye contact and eye movement, posture and movement, proxemics, and prosody" (p. 11), which may assist them to become better communicators in additional languages as well as in their mother tongue.

Summary

In this chapter I have argued that a drama approach to foreign language pedagogy synthesises various activities and methods which tap into recent research on second language acquisition, taking into account fundamental elements in learning a second language such as comprehensible input, contextualised language, interaction and collaboration, and opportunities for negotiating meaning. Getting meaning across requires not only linguistic expressions but also paralinguistic signals. The latter, however, is often neglected in the traditional second language classroom. The physical nature of drama activities can enable teachers to go beyond the teaching of disembodied language and promote children's spontaneous use of tones of voice and body language.

References

Almond, M. (2005). *Teaching English with drama: How to use drama and plays when teaching.* London: Modern English Publishing.

Baldwin, P., & Fleming, K. (2003). *Teaching literacy through drama.* London: RoutledgeFalmer.

The British Council-Hornby seminars in English language teaching (2006). Retrieved from www.british-council.org/learning-teaching-hornby-seminars-india-2006.doc

Brown, H. D. (2001). *Teaching by principles: An interactive approach to language pedagogy* (2nd ed.). New York: Longman.

Byron, K. (1986). *Drama in the English classroom.* London: Methuen.

Cameron, L. (2001). *Teaching languages to young learners.* Cambridge: Cambridge University Press.

Corden, R. (2000). *Literacy and learning through talk: Strategies for the primary classroom.* Buckingham: Open University Press.

Cremin, T., Goouch, K., Blakemore, L., Goff, E., & Macdonald, R. (2006). Connecting drama and writing: Seizing the moment to write. *Research in Drama Education, 11,* 273–291.

Cremin, T., & Schneider, J. J. (2002). Writing together from within: A cross study analysis of children's writing from five classrooms using process drama. *Research in Drama Education, 7*(1), 61–79.

Culham, C. R. (2002). Coping with obstacles in drama-based ESL teaching: A non-verbal approach. In G. Bräuer (Ed.), *Body and language: Intercultural learning through drama* (pp. 95–112). Westport, CT: Ablex Publishing.

Donaldson, M. (1978). *Children's minds.* London: Croom Helm.

Donoghue, M. R., & Kunkle, J. F. (1979). *Second languages in primary education.* Rowley: Newbury House.

Evans, T. (1984). *Drama in English teaching.* London: Croom Helm.

Grainger, T. (2004). Drama and writing: Enlivening their prose. In P. Goodwin (Ed.), *Literacy through creativity* (pp. 91–104). London: David Fulton.

Grainger, T. (2005). Motivating children to write with purpose and passion. In P. Goodwin (Ed.), *The literate classroom* (pp. 79–89). London: David Fulton.

Halliday, M. A. K. (1970). Language structure and language function. In J. Lyons (Ed.), *New horizons in linguistics* (pp. 140–165). Harmondsworth: Penguin.

Halliday, M. A. K. (1978). *Language as social semiotic: The social interpretation of language and meaning.* London: Edward Arnold.

Halliday, M. A. K., & Hasan, R. (1985). *Language, context, and text: Aspects of language in a social-semiotic perspective.* Victoria: Deakin University.

Kao, S.-M., & O'Neill, C. (1998). *Words into worlds: Learning a second language through process drama.* London: Ablex Publishing.

Kempe, A., & Holroyd, J. (2004). *Speaking, listening and drama.* London: David Fulton.

Kress, G., & Van Leeuwen, T. (2006). *Reading images: The grammar of visual design* (2nd ed.). London: Routledge.

Liu, J. (2002). Process drama in second-and foreign-language classrooms. In G. Bräuer (Ed.), *Body and language: Intercultural learning through drama* (pp. 51–70). Westport, CT: Ablex Publishing.

Neelands, J. (1984). *Making sense of drama: A guide to classroom practice.* London: Heinemann Educational.

Neelands, J. (2004). *Beginning drama 11–14* (2nd ed.). London: David Fulton.

Nicholson, H. (2000). Drama, literacies and difference. In E. Bearne, & V. Watson (Eds.), *Where texts and children meet* (pp. 113–122). London: Routledge.

O'Toole, J. (2008). Process, dialogue and performance: The dramatic art of English teaching. In M. Anderson, J. Hughes, & J. Manuel (Eds.), *Drama and English teaching: Imagination, action and engagement* (pp. 13–31). South Melbourne: Oxford University Press.

Packwood, A., & Messenheimer, T. (2003). Back to the future: Developing children as writers. In E. Bearne, H. Dombey, & T. Grainger (Eds.), *Classroom interactions in literacy* (pp. 144–153). Maidenhead: Open University Press.

Pascoe, R., Mel, M., Walker, P., Ifopo, E., O'Farrell, L., & Karpinin, T. (2004). Drama in the Pacific curriculum. *NJ (Drama Australia Journal), 28*(1), 121–129.

Podlozny, A. (2000). Strengthening verbal skills through the use of classroom drama: A clear link. *Journal of Aesthetic Education, 34*(3/4), 239–275.

Rastelli, L. R. (2006). Drama in language learning. *Encuentro, 16,* 82–94.

Reid, J. (1991). Children's reading. In R. Grieve & M. Hughes (Eds.), *Understanding children: Essays in honour of Margaret Donaldson* (pp. 71–93). Oxford: Basil Blackwell.

Somers, J. (1994). *Drama in the curriculum.* London: Cassell.

Steele, S. (2003). First persons: Writing and role at key stage two. In M. Barrs (Ed.), *The best of language matters* (pp. 182–185). London: Centre for Literacy in Primary Education.

Wagner, B. J. (1998). *Educational drama and language arts: What research shows.* Portsmouth, NH: Heinemann.

Winston, J. (2004). *Drama and English at the heart of the curriculum: Primary and middle years.* London: David Fulton.

Winston, J., & Tandy, M. (2009). *Beginning drama 4–11* (3rd ed.). Oxford: Routledge.

2

Using Stories and Drama to Teach English as a Foreign Language at Primary Level

Li-Yu Sabina Chang and Joe Winston

One of the knotty problems that most primary English teachers in Taiwan have been wrestling with is teaching children with various English learning backgrounds in the same class. It is not uncommon to see children with higher levels of language proficiency respond to their teachers half-heartedly since they have already learned what they are taught, mostly, if not completely, outside school. For those who fall behind, they find the lesson beyond their grasp so their minds wander. This results in a low level of student participation in class and intensifies teachers' frustrations. This chapter proposes a model to help solve such problems by introducing story-based drama for young foreign language learners.

The research was carried out in a public primary school in the northern part of Taiwan. An entire class consisting of a total of thirty-two fifth graders (sixteen girls and sixteen boys, aged between eleven and twelve) participated in the study. While nearly half of the class were in their first or second year of learning English, twelve pupils had already taken English classes outside school for more than four years. The pupils had limited opportunities and no immediate need to use English outside school. An eight-week scheme of work was developed on the basis of the story of Little Red Riding Hood and taught in two forty-minute sessions weekly. The story was chosen for three main reasons. First, it is a popular story that most children in Taiwan have heard. Children's familiarity with stories in their mother tongue may provide the foundation for their comprehension when hearing the same story told in a foreign language. Second, the text of the story, adapted from a jazz chant version written by Carolyn Graham (2003, pp. 17–31), is composed of highly repetitive and rhythmic language elements, which help to reinforce children's language retention and encourage their participation. Third, the story of Little Red Riding Hood has been told and retold in many different styles and versions. The possibility of bringing various endings to this story offers children ample space for creativity and imagination and hence a motivation to use the target language.

Story-based drama for teaching children English

Stories play a significant part in young children's lives. Not only do they learn about the world around them through stories, but above all, they build up a foundation for future learning as well. Research has shown that there is a strong association between children's success in school and their experience with storybooks and storytelling in their mother tongue from an early age. In his longitudinal study, Wells (1985) found that all the children who outperformed on the Knowledge of Literacy tests had stories read or told to them before they started their formal education. With regard to the significance of stories in children's literacy development, Wray and Medwell (1991) maintain that most of the new vocabulary children pick up in their school years is acquired through stories they read or listen to.

The benefits of stories to a child's first language acquisition have been well established. But can the use of stories facilitate young learners' foreign language learning, too? On the subject of the increasing popularity of stories in EFL classrooms, the answer seems positive. Numerous claims have been made about the advantages of learning English through stories. Gerngross (2001), for instance, points out that stories in a foreign language are "an important source of language experience and help children to assimilate and process the language holistically" (p. 194). Kirsch (2008) argues that stories, serving as a good starting point for developing all four language skills, help to foster a child's concentration span and learning strategies. To meet the teachers' need for integrating stories into their English teaching, a number of commercial coursebook writers have produced teaching materials, such as *Playway to English* (Gerngross & Puchta, 2009), *English Land* (Nakamura & Seino, 2006), *New Chatterbox* (Strange, 2006), and *Hip Hip Hooray* (Eisele, Eisele, Hanlon, Hanlon, & Hojel, 2004), which include a variety of stories as a framework for unit planning. Nor is it difficult to find resource books with detailed guidance on the use of stories in the primary English lesson (Ellis & Brewster, 1991, 2002; Hester, 1983; Wright, 1995, 1997).

Storytelling and drama share similar features. To quote Winston (2000), "Drama is essentially a form of communal story sharing" (p. x). However, there also exist some differences between them. Booth and Barton (2000) acknowledge that simply recounting the plot does not create drama. What is essential when combining story and drama is that "there must be a new discovery, a new learning, for drama to be happening during the enactment of a story" (p. 81). The value of story re-enactment lies in children living through key events of the story by taking on roles to interact with others. They work collectively to make sense of the story, and the process of working together allows them to see how everyone thinks in a similar or different way. It is the images created in drama that unlock the meaning and heart of the story and turn them into part of the children's cognitive framework. The journey of exploring stories in a dramatic world is intended to motivate children to use the target language to argue, to persuade, to plead, and to negotiate. After the journey, it is likely that they will become eager to read the printed text because their multi-sensory engagement with the story has paved the way for reading. To develop effectively young learners' English language proficiency, Hughes (2001) suggests:

In general, activities for young language learners will be more successful if they are contextualized and related to the learners. It is also helpful if they combine both verbal and non-verbal language, and linked to immediate and visible action. Furthermore they should be purposeful and real, meaningfully repetitive, and recycle a great deal of language.

(p. 22)

Viewed in this way, story-based drama can be seen as a suitable approach to beginning-level foreign language classes.

In the following section, we will use narrative strategies to depict the teaching process, interweaving classroom vignettes, quotations or dialogues from interviews, and children's work. By doing so, we hope that readers will gain a full and clear picture of this teaching project.

The teaching process

Get physical

The first lesson began with a physical warm-up activity in which the children needed to demonstrate physically proper reactions to given commands. To link the warm-up activity to the story of Little Red Riding Hood, Sabina told the class to imagine that they were trees in a magic forest and could move their branches (i.e. their arms) in different directions as commanded such as right, left, up, down, front, and back. She then paired up the pupils, one acting as a tree, the other as a command-giver. After practising for a few minutes, the class were told that these trees in the magic forest always attempted to grab people walking by with their movable branches. Without hesitation, children instantly started to play in the forest. They would sing "La la la la la! You can't catch me!" and try to dodge the swinging branches when going through it. If someone got caught by the tree, it would shout "Got you!" The purpose of the physical warm-up was to lighten the atmosphere and boost playfulness as conducive to better interaction.

Read the props

Before beginning to tell the story, Sabina then showed the class three props – a basket, a mask of a wolf, and a red cloak with a hood – asking them to try to describe the props in English. The children particularly liked the red cloak, asking if they could try it on. In fact, in the following lessons whenever she needed someone to take on the role of Little Red Riding Hood, she never lacked pupils, either boys or girls, eager to take on this task as they had fun wearing the red cloak. As Dickinson and Neelands (2006) argue, "Objects, or props, have a special value in drama. They are read as having a symbolic importance" (p. 69) and they also "help create the central mood or atmosphere within the story" (p. 77). The red cloak worked like a charm, enticing the children to enter into the world of Little Red Riding Hood.

Meet the roles

In the next exercise, Sabina drew the outline of Little Red Riding Hood and the big bad wolf on two large pieces of paper and placed them on the floor. The children were asked to think about these two characters' physical appearance, age, and temperament. The following questions were used to elicit their oral responses:

- Does Little Red Riding Hood have short/long/straight/curly hair?
- What colour is her hair?
- Does she have big eyes?
- How old is she?
- Is she a good or bad girl? Why?
- Does the wolf look ugly/cute/friendly/mean?
- Is he a good or bad wolf? Why?
- What does he like to eat?

As a take-home assignment, the pupils needed to write a short description of Little Red Riding Hood and the wolf and they expressed their personal views about the characters by responding to the questions asked in class.

"Little Red Riding Hood is a happy girl. The wolf is sad and hungry."

"Little Red Riding Hood may be 8 years old. She is a good girl. She is short and thin. The wolf is a bad wolf. It is a stupid wolf."

"The wolf will not eat boys. It likes to eat girls."

This writing assignment aimed to allow more able children to display the full range of their language ability and apply what they had learned to completing the task, as the example below illustrates:

"Little Red Riding Hood has a beautiful cloak. It is red. She wears it every day."

"Little Red Riding Hood is brave because she sees the wolf but she isn't afraid."

Little Red Riding Hood is seven years old. She is pretty."

"The wolf is bad. It likes to eat people and meat, but the wolf is thin. I think the wolf is the magic wolf. The wolf is very ferocious and dangerous so finally it died."

Tell the story

In our story, there is a girl. Her name is Little Red Riding Hood. She lives with her Mama by the forest. Little Red Riding Hood is a good girl. She listens to her Mama, most of the time. When Mama says, "Go," she goes. When Mama says, "Come," she comes. When Mama says, "Sit," she sits. When Mama says, "Sleep," she sleeps. She is a good girl. She listens to her Mama, most of the time.

The above paragraph is the first part of the story and contains a mixture of narrative and dialogue. The interweaving of narrative and dialogue in a story, according to Cameron (2001), "does much to create its particular atmosphere" (p. 165). She maintains that the time-frame within stories distinguishes the use of verb tenses; that is, the past tense is normally seen in narrative to describe what happened, while in dialogues characters can use any tenses which suit the context of their talk. She adds that in simplified English stories the simple present tense is commonly chosen for narrative, which she regrets, as it deprives learners "of opportunities to hear authentic uses of past tense forms, and the contrast with other tenses, in the meaningful contexts of stories" (p. 166).

Though well argued, the notion of exposing learners to varied verb tense forms in stories is not without its limitations when applied to teaching English as a foreign language to beginners. Especially for learners who speak Chinese as their native tongue, it can be a difficult task to mark the past tense in the initial stage of learning English. Since in Mandarin Chinese tense is not indicated in the verb itself, Chinese EFL learners have a tendency to rely on temporal adverbials to refer to past time. Some pupils in this project were still struggling with basic English grammar, for example subject-verb agreement and the present progressive tense. It was not uncommon to hear them say "He *go* to school by bus" or "I am *eat* breakfast now." Introducing the past tense to them might add a burden to their learning. Therefore, Sabina decided to use the simple present tense to narrate the following story, and the pupils would also be able to focus more on the story content and vocabulary.

The story was told with finger puppets. Satchwell and De Silva (1995) recognise the value of puppets in the foreign language classroom because they are "a colourful and enjoyable way to introduce unknown vocabulary and structures" and "can bring a new dimension to lessons" (p. 28). There were several "wows" from the children when they saw the finger puppet of Little Red Riding Hood for the first time and it certainly served to hold their attention – they were all ears during the storytelling. Sabina then wrote the paragraph on the whiteboard and led the class to read it out loud. Reading aloud, as suggested by Cameron (2001), benefits children's language development in a number of ways. She argues that:

> reading aloud familiarises children with the language of written English: the formulaic openings (*Once upon a time …*) and closings (*and so they all lived happily after*); the patterns of text types – stories and information texts, and sentence types. Affectively, reading aloud can motivate children to want to read themselves.
>
> (p. 141)

On the other hand, she emphasises the necessity of making sure that children grasp the overall meaning of the text and the majority of words in it. To prevent young learners from falling into the trap of merely barking at the print, she urges that the teacher offer them a "skeleton" to build on their understanding of the text by using, for instance, "pictures that show characters and action, and by talking about the text in advance and giving enough of the meaning" (p. 141). The way the pupils were helped to make connections between words and meaning in this lesson was mainly by means of body language. With each repeated reading aloud, Sabina rubbed out some words and used gestures to aid their recall. In the end, most of the children were able to memorise and speak out the whole paragraph with the aid of her physical prompts.

Act it out

The narrator plays a crucial part in drama and storytelling. Winston (2004) states that narration can be exploited to "introduce, link or conclude action," "slow and intensify action," "mark the passage of time," or "introduce the next stage of a drama" (p. 142). Sabina briefly told the class the function of a narrator in stories, a role that moves the story forward by telling, but not acting, part of the story line and whose attitude towards and interpretation of the events or characters can influence how the reader or audience perceives the story. She also demonstrated different dramatic effects created by where narrators position themselves on stage. So, for example, a narrator who stands elevated behind the characters looks like a puppet master, whereas if she sits herself on the floor in front of them they look as though they emerge like thoughts from her head. The pupils were then divided into groups of four to act out the story by taking on roles of narrators and characters (one as Little Red Riding Hood, another one as Mama, and the other two as narrators). In their group presentations, the children creatively showed different relationships between Little Red Riding Hood and her mother. One boy, for example, played a very bossy mother who gave commands such as "Go", "Come", "Sit", "Sleep" with gestures like those we use when manipulating a puppet. One girl, by contrast, was a gentle mother who spoke softly to her daughter, played by another girl who pretended to be rebellious, pouting her lips, shrugging her shoulders, and stamping her feet to show her unwillingness to follow her mother's commands. As the narrator said the last sentence, "*She listens to her mama most of the time*", she made an ironic face and stuck out her tongue at her mother.

Watching others act out the story enhances the learners' memorisation and provides a meaningful context for the vocabulary taught. In this lesson, the story was acted out by eight groups of children in eight different ways, reinforcing memorisation and understanding of the content. When Sabina interviewed the children later, one pupil said to her, "Being an audience also helps me learn English because I not only listen to but also watch the story." Her opinion was supported by other children:

SABINA: Do you like watching others act out the story?
ALL: Yes. It's fun!
BOY 1: It makes me laugh.
SABINA: Do you think making you laugh is important for you in terms of learning English?
BOY 2: Yes. Gotta learn happily.
BOY 1: Right. And I can remember better.
BOY 3: I can hear the dialogues much more times through watching others perform and it helps me learn English better.

[Note: All the interviews were conducted in Mandarin Chinese and the interview extracts are translated into English by Sabina.]

In fact, after one month the co-teacher was surprised to find that the children were still able to recite by heart the narrative together with a dialogue which we will describe in the next section. After class, she gave her comments as follows:

It's really amazing! It's been quite a long while since you taught them that part of the story. And we even had a spring break in between. But they still remember! I think it's because the pupils had the chance to act it out in groups and watching their classmates perform has become a great language input for them. It impressed them more than passively listening to the CD.

Sing and act

MAMA: (Sung to the tune of Frère Jacques)

Are you sleeping? Are you sleeping? Red Riding Hood. Red Riding Hood. Morning bells are ringing. Morning bells are ringing. Ding ding dong. Ding ding dong.
Get up. Get up. It's time to get up.

LRRH: Oh no. Oh no. I don't want to get up.
MAMA: Come on. Come on. It's time to get up.
LRRH: OK. OK. It's time to get up. Mmmm, something smells like chocolate. Something smells like peanut butter. Chocolate peanut butter cookies? It's chocolate peanut butter cookies!
MAMA: These cookies are for Granny. She's home alone and sick in bed. Please go and see her this morning.
LRRH: Oh, poor Granny. She's sick and all-alone. I'll go and see her this morning.

The dialogue above begins with a song sung to the tune of Frère Jacques, a melody which is so well known that the class soon joined in and sang along. Young learners enjoy music and rhythm. It is easier for them to remember words in a song or a chant than in a spoken text. Story and drama provide rich contexts for teachers to incorporate songs into their lessons, which, in turn, may add a dramatic feel to the storytelling and acting out. The pupils were put into groups of four to enact the dialogue. To lower their anxiety level about having to learn the dialogue by heart, Sabina informed them that two members in the group would be prompters, reading out the dialogue line by line for the other two members to repeat and act out. The prompters had to recognise the words in advance and pronounce them clearly while the actors were required to grasp what had been said and reproduce the sentence accompanied by proper tones, facial expressions, and gestures in order to show their comprehension.

Miming and finger puppet show

MAMA: Little Red Riding Hood, please sit down and listen to me carefully.
LRRH: Yes, Mama. I'm listening.
MAMA: Go straight to Granny's house.
LRRH: Yes, Mama. I will.
MAMA: Don't talk to strangers.
LRRH: No, Mama. I won't.
MAMA: Be very careful.
LRRH: Yes, Mama. I will.
MAMA: All right. Take this basket and go to your granny now.
LRRH: Bye-bye, Mama.
MAMA: Bye-bye, my dear.

To assist the children's comprehension of the above dialogue, Sabina chose some sentences to mime without telling the class which ones they were. The pupils then needed to guess the mimed sentence. The value of incorporating mime in second language classrooms has been underscored by Kao and O'Neill (1998) who comment that "mime is an alternative for L2 learners at lower competence levels to express their thoughts with their body and not in the language that they are not yet comfortable with" (p. 30). When Sabina mimed, the children all looked at her with concentration, trying to match her movements with the sentences in the dialogue and hastily shouting out their answers. Some children even asked if they could do the miming themselves. Those who volunteered included a number of pupils whose English proficiency was deficient and yet who still found this activity engaging and entertaining.

The pupils were asked to make their own finger puppets to re-enact the dialogue. In recent years there has been a growing interest in the use of puppetry for educational purposes. Language teachers, in particular, can benefit from using puppets in the classroom. Phillips (1999) views puppets as "a very versatile resource in the young learners' classroom". She claims:

> Children use language while making them, often respond to puppets more readily than to the teacher, and are usually enthusiastic about manipulating them. The process of making a puppet is a rewarding craft activity itself and the end product, the puppet, plays a key role in a subsequent activity.
>
> (p. 51)

With simple instructions given, the pupils made their own finger puppets at home for fear of taking up limited class time. Some of the children's work is shown in Figure 2.1. To be more environmentally friendly, several pupils used cartons or recycled paper in their puppet making (Figure 2.1 A–D). A couple of the children even drew a simple backdrop for their performance. One girl's backdrop (Figure 2.1 H) was a creative one – with a window cut out of the house, letting the finger puppets appear from within. The class appreciated her idea, which was a great encouragement to her since she had never been the centre of attention in this class before due to her poor English performance.

Sabina encouraged the pupils to experiment with all kinds of voices and tones to present Little Red Riding Hood and her mother. For example, Little Red Riding Hood can sound impatient because she is annoyed by her mother's nagging. Or she can speak in a frightened voice as she needs to go through the forest to visit her granny on her own. The finger puppet show brought out different aspects of the pupils' personalities and classroom behaviour. In her journal Sabina wrote:

> Richard becomes excitable and distracted very easily. He often uses over-exaggerated body language to draw attention from others without realising that his gestures can sometimes be inappropriate. Particularly for some girls in this class who seem more mature at their age, his behaviour is "a bit childish and weird". Nevertheless, he acted quite surprisingly well when presenting with finger puppets today. Hiding behind the backdrop, he could only focus on his manipulation of the finger puppet and express himself through his voice. He spoke so fluently and clearly that the class gave him a big hand at the end of his performance. He looked overjoyed. After class, he came to tell me that he felt a sense of achievement, which he had never experienced before in previous English classes.

FIGURE 2.1 Examples of children's finger puppets A–H

Story circle

The story circle, also known as "whoosh" or "story wand", is a theatrical ensemble in which children spontaneously act out different roles responding to the narration in the acting space within the circle. The other children sitting in the circle with no specific roles assigned make up the audience watching the performance and helping to create sound effects or chant repetitive phrases. The narrator retells the story by waving a "story wand" to assign those who volunteer to enact the mentioned roles to enter the acting space and perform. During the process of storytelling, the narrator can wave the stick over the acting area to indicate the clearance of space and invite new volunteers to act out the remaining scenes. To assist the student actors to respond properly to the narration with facial expression, gesture, posture, and tone of voice, the storyteller needs to re-adapt the text, providing more detailed description about physical actions. Through re-enacting the story in the story circle, children are able to "go over the events of the plot in a way that stealthily re-enforces their recall of it" (Winston, 2009, p. 39). Additionally, their spontaneous physicality can be conducive to varying the pace of teaching and refocusing attention.

What Sabina narrated in the story circle was based on all the dialogues taught previously and the English dialogue below, with a bridging narration added to describe how Little Red Riding Hood had fun playing with animals in the forest, totally forgetting her mother's warnings.

After walking into the forest, Little Red Riding Hood sees many cute animals. She has so much fun playing with them that she forgets what her mother has told her: Go straight to Granny's house. Don't talk to strangers. Be careful.

And here comes the Wolf!

WOLF: *(Hides behind the tree.) What a lucky day! I'll have something yummy for my hungry tummy.*

(Walks to LRRH.) Good morning, my dear. I'm Mr. Wolf. How are you this morning?

TREES: *Don't tell! Don't tell! Don't talk to strangers!*
LRRH: *I'm fine, thank you, Mr. Wolf. How are you?*
WOLF: *(Smiles) Just fine, my dear. What's your name?*
LRRH: *My name is Little Red Riding Hood.*
TREES: *Oh, really? You're Little Red Riding Hood. Everyone says you're a good girl.*
LRRH: *Oh, really?*
WOLF: *Oh, yes! Everyone says you're a nice little girl.*
LRRH: *Thank you, Mr. Wolf. You're very nice.*
WOLF: *(Smells something.) Do I smell cookies?*
TREES: *Don't tell! Don't tell! Don't talk to strangers.*
LRRH: *Yes, it's chocolate peanut butter cookies for Granny. She's home alone and sick in bed. I'm going to see her.*
WOLF: *What a nice little girl! Where does your granny live?*
TREES: *Don't tell! Don't tell! Don't talk to strangers.*
LRRH: *Granny lives in the little red house over there.*
WOLF: *I know that house. I have an idea. Look at the beautiful flowers over there. Why don't you pick some flowers for Granny?*

> TREES: *Don't stop! Don't stop! Go straight to Granny's house!*
> LRRH: *That's a good idea! Thank you, Mr. Wolf.*
> WOLF: *You're welcome. Bye-bye, my dear.*
> LRRH: *Bye-bye, Mr. Wolf.*

After introducing the story wand to the children, Sabina started to narrate the story by saying, "In our story there is a girl. Her name is Little Red Riding Hood." Then she paused, waiting for any volunteer to take the role. The children hesitated, not sure what would happen in the acting space. A few seconds passed as they whispered to each other before Ethan put up his hand. Sabina pointed the stick at him and he entered the acting space. The text below is drawn from Sabina's journal:

[Note: Text in *italics* indicates words or sentences *originally spoken in English*.]

"Hello, everybody. My name is Little Red Riding Hood. I'm a good girl. I listen to my mama most of the time," said Ethan loud and clear without any prompt from me. His pretending to be a good girl made everyone laugh, which also swept away the children's hesitation. Therefore when I said, *"There are many trees in the forest,"* a few hands quickly rose. I pointed at Victor, saying, *"This is a tall tree."* He repeated after me, standing upright with his arms reaching up high. I continued, *"This tree is taller than that tree,"* signalling to Sam to be the taller one. Sam is actually a little shorter than Victor but he responded to my narration without thinking too much – standing on his toes and stretching his arms even higher than Victor when saying, *"I'm taller than that tree."* I next introduced to the audience a very thin tree which was played by Terry, who quietly tightened himself up and drew in his arms and legs while repeating my sentence in a squeaky voice. He even held his breath and squeezed his face into a narrow and wrinkled mass, trying to look as thin as possible. Being a big tree, Richard made an interesting contrast by spreading his arms and legs wide open, roaring, *"I'm a big tree."*

In the later part of the story, when the Wolf suggested that Little Red Riding Hood pick some flowers for Granny, Sabina had several pupils come into the acting space, pretending to be various kinds of flower – cute, shy, happy, sad, and so on. Posing in different gestures, they all yelled, "Pick me! Pick me!" As Winston and Tandy (2009) argue, physically creating the scenery of the story, apart from being fun, introduces children "to the importance of the body in drama, to how it can represent a myriad of symbolic meanings, and develops their confidence in improvising spontaneously with their bodies" (p. 30). When the trees chanted warnings to Little Red Riding Hood, the audience joined in too. Sabina encouraged them to vary their tone of voice to caution the little girl to avoid the Wolf and show their feelings about seeing her walking into the Wolf's trap without even knowing it. They whispered. They shouted. They sounded worried, scared, anxious, and angry. Their chorus established a theatrical feel that can seldom be experienced when merely role-playing dialogues drawn from a textbook.

Picture book storytelling

To offer the children an opportunity to see how visual and aural aids work together to enrich the written text, Sabina chose Nicoletta Ceccoli's (2004) picture book to retell the story of *Little Red Riding Hood* as the last classroom activity in this scheme

25

FIGURE 2.2 Illustrations from picture books made by children

of work. As an award-winning illustrator, Ceccoli portrays the little girl and the wolf in an unusual way with a vibrant, sleek illustrative style which is artistically impressive. After the storytelling, Sabina shared with the class Roald Dahl's (1982) well-known poem, "Little Red Riding Hood and the Wolf" from his collection of *Revolting Rhymes*. Although they needed her translation to understand the content, the pupils were surprised by the ending in which the cunning Little Miss Red Riding Hood shot Wolfie dead with a pistol before turning him into a "lovely furry wolfskin coat". Traditional tales lend themselves to use in an EFL classroom because of their potential for rewriting and children's familiarity with the story content. Barton and Booth (1990) rightly point out that "When we add to the story, continue the story, or write epilogues for the story, or rewrite the ending, the children are involved in shared authorship" (p. 97).

Making a mini storybook was the pupils' last written task in this scheme of work. They were told that the storybook should consist of a book cover and six content pages, presenting the key moments in the story. The pupils were required to illustrate each page with a picture drawn from any of the images they had seen or created during the drama activities in class. One boy's work, as shown in Figure 2.2, for instance, incorporated a scene in which a group had shown Little Red Riding Hood's mother using a broom to persuade her lazy daughter to get out of bed. The horns on the mother's head and the way she is jumping up high to strike a heavy blow express her anger in a vivid and comical manner. It is also testimony to the strength of the impression that a visual enactment can have on a child.

FIGURE 2.3 Illustrations from picture books made by children

FIGURE 2.4 Illustrations from picture books made by children

FIGURE 2.5 Illustrations from picture books made by children

As the children's English learning experiences and proficiency levels varied considerably, two writing tasks were given for them to choose from. Those who did not feel confident enough in their writing ability were allowed to copy the phrases or sentences from the dialogues or narrations taught in class to match their illustrations. Those who wanted to challenge their imaginations could rewrite the story with a different ending. In one girl's version, Red Riding Hood was not a girl but a little wolf. In the forest, she meets a big bad girl who is actually a wolf eater. Like Eugene Trivizas's *The Three Little Wolves and the Big Bad Pig*, the characters in her retelling are in reverse, with a little wolf that looks innocent and harmless, contrasting with the giant, menacing girl. In another boy's story, Granny became the heroine, tricking the wolf into eating a human-shaped toy which looks exactly like her. Eventually, she knocks the wolf dead with a proud smile. Another boy's story (see Figures 2.3–5) blends Roald Dahl's *Little Red Riding Hood and the Wolf* into a local and contemporary setting, in which the pistol–packing girl happily cycles to the 7–11, the most popular convenience store in Taiwan, witnesses the wolf's attack on people, and bravely shoots him dead. Her wolfskin cloak sends a warning to the other wolves, so that they dare not bully her grandmother any more. Within only six pages, this boy retold the story with strongly crafted pictures and a high level of literary composition. In the end–of–term interview, he said, "I think the written assignment is important in terms of improving my English. Simply copying vocabulary words is very boring. I prefer more challenging homework such as letter writing and making mini books." His remarks point to the need to provide differentiated writing tasks for mixed ability classes.

Conclusion

This scheme of work has illustrated how to incorporate story-based drama into primary English instruction and has offered empirical evidence of its impact on children's learning. The majority of the participants reported in an end-of-term questionnaire that they had made progress in their four language skills – listening, speaking, reading, and writing. With only one pupil expressing a neutral view, the rest of the class indicated that they liked learning English through drama and stories. They also agreed that drama and stories make English learning easier. The pupils' various types of written work and in-class drama presentations demonstrated a noticeable improvement in their English language abilities, evidence that projects such as this can lead to positive learning outcomes for children with different levels of English language proficiency.

One of the challenges of mixed ability classes that primary teachers of English need to overcome is how to encourage participation. With the use of stories and drama, many of the pupils in this project were drawn out of their silence into more active classroom participation. They enjoyed physical activities, performing for others and watching others' performances. How children feel in the classroom determines their willingness to participate in activities. Drama requires active participation from attendees, so it is essential for teachers to create an atmosphere of trust and playfulness conducive to boosting co-operation, collaboration, and interaction. Moreover, it is worth stressing that, through participating in drama activities, children have abundant opportunities to notice and respond to the non-verbal aspects of language which are often neglected in language classrooms. Many pupils in this study mentioned their enjoyment at being able to use gestures and tone of voice to indicate their feelings and attitudes when acting out the story. They are unlikely to gain such learning experiences from reading the traditional textbook dialogues which are typically function-orientated and bear little relation to children's emotional and physical engagement. Most importantly, this study shows that story-based drama provides a variety of learning modalities to accommodate varying learner styles and characteristics. It also enables children with different levels of English proficiency to co-operate and contribute to group work on an equal basis.

References

Barton, B., & Booth, D. (1990). *Stories in the classroom: Storytelling, reading aloud and roleplaying with children*. Ontario: Pembroke.

Booth, D., & Barton, B. (2000). *Story works: How teachers can use shared stories in the new curriculum*. Ontario: Pembroke.

Cameron, L. (2001). *Teaching languages to young learners*. Cambridge: Cambridge University Press.

Ceccoli, N. (2004). *Little Red Riding Hood*. Bath: Barefoot Books.

Dickinson, R., & Neelands, J. (2006). *Improve your primary school through drama*. London: David Fulton.

Eisele, B., Eisele, C.Y., Hanlon, R.Y., Hanlon, S. M., & Hojel, B. (2004). *Hip hip hooray*. London: Longman.

Ellis, G., & Brewster, J. (1991). *The storytelling handbook for primary teachers*. London: Penguin.

Ellis, G., & Brewster, J. (2002). *Tell it again! The new storytelling handbook for primary teachers*. Harlow: Pearson Education.

Gerngross, G. (2001). Fascinating children: Using stories in teaching English as a foreign language in a first-year primary class. In M. Jiménez Raya, P. Faber, W. Gewehr, & A. J. Peck (Eds.), *Effective foreign language teaching at the primary level: Focus on the teacher* (pp. 187–194). Oxford: Peter Lang.

Gerngross, G., & Puchta, H. (2009). *Playway to English*. Cambridge: Cambridge University Press.

Graham, C. (2003). *Jazz chant fairy tales*. New York: Oxford University Press.

Hester, H. (1983). *Stories in the multilingual primary classroom: Supporting children's learning of English as a second language*. London: Inner London Education Authority.

Hughes, A. (2001). The teaching of language to young learners: Linking understanding and principles with practice. In M. Jiménez Raya, P. Faber, W. Gewehr, & A. J. Peck (Eds.), *Effective foreign language teaching at the primary level: Focus on the teacher* (pp. 17–24). New York: Peter Lang.

Kao, S.-M., & O'Neill, C. (1998). *Words into worlds: Learning a second language through process drama*. London: Ablex Publishing.

Kirsch, C. (2008). *Teaching foreign languages in the primary school*. London: Continuum.

Nakamura, M., & Seino, A. (2006). *English land*. New York: Pearson Longman.

Phillips, S. (1999). *Drama with children*. Oxford: Oxford University Press.

Satchwell, P., & De Silva, J. (1995). *Catching them young*. London: Centre for Information on Language Teaching & Research.

Strange, D. (2006). *New chatterbox*. New York: Oxford University Press.

Wells, G. (1985). *Language, learning and education: Selected papers from the bristol study 'language at home and at school'*. Windsor: NFER-Nelson.

Winston, J. (2000). *Drama, literacy and moral education 5–11*. London: David Fulton.

Winston, J. (2004). *Drama and English at the heart of the curriculum: Primary and middle years*. London David Fulton.

Winston, J. (2009). Beauty, laughter and the charming virtues of drama. *Drama Research. International journal of drama in education, 1*, 38–45.

Winston, J., & Tandy, M. (2009). *Beginning drama 4–11* (3rd ed.). Oxford: Routledge.

Wray, D., & Medwell, J. (1991). *Literacy and language in the primary years*. London: Routledge.

Wright, A. (1995). *Storytelling with children*. Oxford: Oxford University Press.

Wright, A. (1997). *Creating stories with children*. Oxford: Oxford University Press.

3

Theatre, Language Learning and Identity (1)

Empowering Additional Language Learners through Theatre in Education

Deborah Hull

Introduction

The Play House is a UK based theatre education charity that has twenty-five years experience of delivering a range of participatory drama and theatre projects with children and young people from Birmingham and the West Midlands. Much of the company's work takes place in culturally diverse educational settings where pupils speak many languages. As a response to the diversity of its participants the company has previously developed work using culturally specific stories and art forms, experimented with the integration of community languages into its performances and employed practitioners from a range of cultural backgrounds. However despite the fact that the company was originally set up to support children from communities newly arrived to the UK, it has itself in recent years moved away from working explicitly within a language agenda.

Re-engaging the company with work that was language-focussed was spurred by the formation nationally of extended school's networks – clusters of schools and educational settings working together to implement a range of out of hours activities to enhance children's and young people's social, recreational and educational opportunities. It was through the identification of the need to support children with English as an Additional Language (EAL) by a local cluster, that The Play House was approached to develop work. The lack of proficiency in English was judged by school leaders to be a barrier to pupils' educational attainment and something for which there were limited resources available. The Play House was not only felt to provide an innovative methodology that could be adapted for classroom use but also to hold essential local knowledge of pupils' needs.

Initially the company negotiated to develop eight, one hour participatory drama and story workshops for a maximum of ten pupils per group from years 1 and 2 (five to seven year olds). These were to constitute pilot sessions and were to take place out of hours in two inner city schools with which The Play House had an established relationship. Each session involved a practitioner from the company working with the support of a teacher or teaching assistant from the school, who would also be responsible for monitoring children's progress. Following the initial piloting period the projects were rolled out to other schools within the cluster and then later to other clusters across the city. To date, similar projects have taken place in fourteen different settings.

The commissioning of the company to create these sessions prompted a period of internal development that involved drawing together the collective insights of its staff, conducting further reading and formulating a clear set of aspirations for the project to complement and deepen the extended schools' language agenda.

Company members held many tacit understandings about the experiences of EAL children and the realities of educating culturally diverse classes. A striking feature of many of the classrooms they visited was that they appeared to be "*English only zone(s)*" (Blackledge & Creese, 2010, p. 45) and that this did not fit with the very real diversity Play House practitioners saw being played out within the wider school community – displays hung in corridors celebrating pupils' cultural heritage, welcome signs in the school reception area written in community languages, conversations conducted on the playground and with parents on the walk to school in Urdu, Panjabi or Arabic. The company found that these observations were mirrored in the theoretical writings of researchers of multilingualism with McCarthy et al. pointing out that despite the United Kingdom being a nation of many peoples and languages, "educational policies and practices often deny that multilingual multicultural reality, attempting to coerce it into a single monolingualist and monoculturalist mould" (Blackledge & Creese, 2010, p. 44).

However, on reading further, it became clear that the impetus behind the exclusive use of English in the classroom did not originate from educational policy alone. Media and political rhetoric has consistently labelled the prevalence of community languages as problematic: "The public discourse has made associations between the visibility of minority languages and societal problems such as civil unrest, social segregation, family break down, educational failure and financial burden to the state" (Blackledge & Creese, 2010, p. 5). Such beliefs have permeated deeply, not only educationally but also socially. But at what cost? Research indicates that the imposition of a strong monolingual culture has had considerable impact – when children are denied opportunities to use their home languages in school they "often internalise ambivalence and shame in relation to their linguistic and cultural heritage" (Blackledge & Creese, 2010, p. 45). Indeed, there is considerable evidence to suggest that rather than children being encouraged to make a speedy transition to English in the classroom, "bilingualism can benefit overall intellectual progress where both languages continue to develop and when children feel they are adding English to their language repertoire" (Primary National Strategy: Excellence and Enjoyment Unit 2).

For The Play House these findings presented a strong case for developing a model of English language learning that looked beyond simple functionality and towards issues of identity and culture. If The Play House was to work within an English language learning agenda and yet not be guilty of pushing children to "internalising ambivalence and shame" then it was apparent that it would have to strive for ways of accommodating, integrating and referencing the use of home languages and culture alongside the promotion and practice of English.

The rest of this chapter is an account of the company's attempts to do this.

Drama and story sessions

The starting point for the sessions was a series of well known stories – Jack and the Beanstalk, King Midas and his Golden Touch, The Selfish Giant and Little Red Riding Hood. These had previously been used by the company and were known to provide rich opportunities for drama work. The initial planning of activities within these stories focused on:

- developing in-role encounters for children that would enable them to speak in a range of social contexts;
- seeking out moments of participation within the stories that would allow children to contribute their own ideas and experiences;
- establishing the ways in which the stories could be conveyed non-verbally;
- finding opportunities for the children to inhabit the stories and play out situations;
- using the stories to embody abstract concepts and language;
- devising "imperatives" within the stories to provide the impetus for children's participation.

These activities were collectively to provide the stimulus for children's use of English, establishing a contextualised and authentic environment in which to speak and listen.

Because of the relatively young age of the children involved in the sessions, the activities needed not only to take into account children's learning within a second language, but also the fact that they were simultaneously gaining proficiency within their first or home language.

Artefacts

Each session began with a story bag or box containing a variety of artefacts relating to the telling of the story that day. Artefacts included: a golden cloth, crown, shoes, cups and toys for the King Midas story; herbs, brightly coloured glass medicine bottles, a basket, pine cones, apples and a red cloak for Little Red Riding Hood; a wooden spoon, an apron, beans, a leather purse, coins and a pair of giant boots for Jack and the Beanstalk; and a large hammer, the giant's jacket, a 'keep out' sign and a basic map of a garden for The Selfish Giant. Children were encouraged to handle, comment on, interrogate, speculate about and then label these in both English and their home languages. Following this a collective decision was taken by the group as to which language would be used to describe the individual objects later when referred to in the story. Over the eight sessions this exploration of artefacts evolved into something of a ritual, signalling an early invitation to children to participate in the story, offering visual clues as to the kind of story that was to take place, allowing a moment of negotiation and ownership and providing children with an emblematic way into the narrative.

Later, when artefacts featured in the context of the story, there were further opportunities for children to build ownership and to develop language around the "objects in action". In the King Midas story, the children each selected an object from the box to present to the King. They were asked to become servants in the royal household with a golden gift for the greedy ruler (played by the practitioner). In preparation they decided on *what* they would say about their artefact and *how* they should speak to the King about it. As they stepped into the story a series of simple, repeated questions were posed by the King to the children, in turn, to allow them the opportunity formally to present their chosen object:

King Midas: My servant, come closer. What is your name? How long have you been working for me in my palace? What do you have for me today? What is it made out of? What does it do/ what is it for? How much is it worth?

A typical response was:

Servant: (Bowing) Your Majesty, My name is xx, I have worked in the palace for ten years. I bring you a clock to tell the time. It is made of gold and is worth a million pounds." (Bowing again)

The children often hid their object behind their back so as to reveal it to the King with great ceremony. They employed a respectful tone and as the activity progressed, often borrowed from and extended what the other children had said.

"It is worth ten million pounds and is all gold."

The practitioner then stepped out of role to pick up on the thread of storytelling and directly accommodate the children's in-role responses into the fabric of the narrative:

"The servants had worked for King Midas for many years, they bowed before him and from behind their backs brought clocks of gold, worth a million pounds ..."

Here a relatively complex task had been made manageable by focussing instruction on a set of tangible objects. In realising the task children were expected to:

- select vocabulary to describe the qualities of an object;
- verbally respond "in the moment";
- use appropriate tone and register within a social discourse outside of their own experience.

These are tasks that the teachers associated with the project had identified as being difficult for EAL children to carry out. But because their efforts were firmly focussed on something they could see, touch and name they were able to engage more confidently and readily with what was being asked of them.

Closely related to the use of artefacts as a means of supporting children's learning was the use of collective drawings. Again during the King Midas story, the children were asked to draw together on a large sheet of paper some of the things King Midas touched in order to turn them to gold. Each child was asked to name what they had drawn and a shared understanding of the object was established through discussion and demonstration. These drawings were then used as a visual script by the practitioner to narrate (using the children's own labels) King Midas enjoying his magic, golden touch. This narrative was simultaneously played out by the children all taking on the role of the King himself going about his palace, touching the imaginary objects in turn. Having such visual markers present in the story allowed those children without sufficient English to follow the storytelling, an alternative visual means of engaging with and acting out the narrative events.

Through framing the stories using artefacts and reintroducing them during key episodes and events in the storytelling, objects became useful tools for recapping and revisiting moments of the narrative – skills that their teachers tell us EAL children often struggle to develop. As children made a visual association between the objects used and the events that had been played out or told within the story, they were more able to recall moments out of sequence and return to earlier sections of the story, using the artefacts as a prompt.

Later sessions of the project saw a shift away from working within established narratives and towards supporting children in the creation of their own original stories. Again the use of artefacts was of central importance here. In these sessions a range of more abstract items was presented to the group (fabric, shells, stones and feathers) and through careful questioning – *who owned them, what they were, what they did* – a loose narrative structure began to emerge. The children were aided in imagining possibilities for their own narratives through their participation in the previous sessions' stories and much of their own storytelling reflected the themes and characters of these earlier stories, with enchanted princesses, kings returning from the dead and magical spells featuring strongly. However, they were also able to draw on more mundane realities: in one session a girl chose some shiny paper from the box which she described as *"snow sprinkled all around"*. She went on to tell a story about a child who built a snowman before dropping to the ground to demonstrate how the child had made the shape of an angel in the snow. The artefact had provided the stimulus for a story that the girl had wanted to share using all the resources she had available to her – she struggled to speak in English, she acted out her story and with greater permission and support she might also have used her home language – this issue of permission is something that will be returned to at the end of the chapter.

What appeared to be taking place here was the idea of "inner story making". The girl had an obvious narrative in her head that she was attempting to externalise and convey to others but seemingly did not have sufficient means of communicating her story. This inner story-making was played out in other sessions – the comments below are taken from a teacher who had been involved in the project and who extended the use of artefacts to her whole class:

> *"We did a circle time – and children represented the objects in any way they chose. After this pupil 1 chose to show her story bag story – she showed her story by moving her objects, flying the bird on – it was obvious she had a story in her head – but she did not speak – but looked very comfortable and proud."*

There are many potential reasons why pupil 1 chose not to verbalise her story; if however it was because she did not have adequate English to articulate her ideas, then this feels like a missed opportunity to support her in using her home language. Working in this way could have allowed her storytelling to become the starting point of a process that progressed from recording and drawing a narrative she had an obvious connection to, towards ultimately translating it into English. Of course the real barrier here is time – time for a lone teacher to see this intensive one to one process through. However, the tensions involved in accommodating bilingualism as an integral part of English language learning must be balanced with the potential impacts of continuing to operate a monolingual learning environment:

> This may make minority language children feel less confident in their cultural background, their language community their home values and beliefs, even less confident of themselves.
>
> (Baker, 2002, p. 405)

One way in which the project was able successfully to support children in using their home languages was by providing each child with his or her own individual storybag containing the same artefacts that were used to generate the original stories. Children were able to take away these bags at the end of the project and were encouraged to use them to share their stories at home with siblings and parents. The anecdotal evidence that came back from teachers and teaching assistants was that children grasped this opportunity and that the artefacts had created a common ground between school and home, for bilingual storytelling.

Story and drama

The project explored a range of traditional tales, ancient myths and stories devised by the children and during the eight sessions a variety of storytelling and drama techniques were employed to encourage and support the children in developing skills in English language speaking and listening. The cornerstone of these sessions was getting pupils to engage with and be excited by the narratives and drawing them into a relationship with the characters. Achieving this effectively motivated them to want to communicate with and about characters, to enter into the story, to play out significant moments of action and to reflect on the people, places and events of the narrative – all activities rich in English language speaking potential.

As the project progressed it became clear that two approaches were starting to yield some success in inducing children to participate – the use of universal story elements and opening up gaps in the narrative.

The use of universal story elements

All of the established stories used in the project came from a European tradition of storytelling – Little Red Riding Hood and Jack and the Beanstalk are well known European fairy stories, King Midas is a Greek myth and The Selfish Giant is one of Oscar Wilde's best loved tales. Despite this, the themes and lessons embedded in the stories are universal, popping up in stories from around the world. Themes such as greed, betrayal, violence, magic, restoration and redemption, and lessons such as respect your parents, be careful what you wish for and treat others as you would wish to be treated yourself. The universality of these themes and lessons allowed children to engage with the stories. They were being offered something that either bore a resemblance to stories they had been previously exposed to at home or in school; or in cases where children had not experienced story-rich environments, the stories crystallised recognisable concepts from life itself.

The themes and issues within the stories were played out through strong, archetypal characters and again this proved useful in establishing for children recognisable codes of behaviour and transaction. During the sessions, children encountered greedy kings, scolding parents, selfish giants, scary ogres, mischievous boys and brave little girls, all of whom operated within predictable parameters. In effect, this provided the children with some "scaffolding" for their interactions with the characters, which circumvented the need for detailed context-setting by the practitioner before children were able to engage in talk with, as and about the characters. Some examples of children responding within clear character frames are included below:

A child in-role as Jack's downtrodden, nagging mum said with a sigh: "I have to do *everything for him.*"

A child taking on the role of a playful Jack when being asked what he can see from the top of the beanstalk replied: "I can see a giant sun and clouds" and "a big cup you could fall into."

A child being asked to recap on the previous week's story when she role-played hiding from the ogre said: *"I was in the clothes and I was scared that if he put on his clothes he would feels [sic] someone in there and would eat me up."*

Another girl in the same session described the ogre's favourite food as being *"chicken kebab with people".*

These snippets reflect the diversity of role-based interactions that the children were asked to participate in during the project. These included the practitioner taking on roles such as:

- The Selfish Giant just after he had erected a large fence and "Keep Out" sign around his garden being questioned by the children as to his motives (see Winston, 2004, p. 59).

- Jack seeking the children's approval for having swapped his mother's cow for five magic beans rather than taking it to market.

In these roles, practitioners could clearly model – through their body language, facial expressions, tone of voice and language employed – a clear sense of which archetypal character they were playing. This served as a means of transmitting to the children "rules of engagement" for the ensuing role play. However, more often than not these in-role encounters involved the children also taking on roles alongside the practitioner:

- Children collectively became Little Red answering questions from her mother, Mrs Hood, about the jobs she had done in the cottage while her mother had been out in the forest collecting herbs.

- Jack's mother asked the children in a collective role as Jack to explain himself after giving away her best cow for a handful of beans.

- The children acted as servants in the royal household presenting King Midas with a variety of foods to eat (of their own choosing) which he touched and accidently turned to gold.

In these instances children were implicated directly into the social context – these ranging from the domestic to the courtly – and required to make use of subject specific vocabulary as well as to practise a variety of different language registers and styles. However, they were aided in this by the fact that each of these encounters had a very clear story imperative behind it which gave impetus to the children's participation, and each featured well defined character types that guided the children in shaping their responses.

One example of this in action was during the King Midas story after he had turned his own children to gold by mistake. The practitioner in role as the King gathered his servants (the children) together to appeal for help in breaking the wish that had given him his golden touch.

My servants, I have been greedy and now I have turned my own children to gold. I need your help. You are clever and will know what to do. How do I make this magic stop?

Referencing earlier sections of the story, the children would make suggestions such as:

"Your majesty, wash your hands in the river."

"You have to find the butterfly (who had given the wish) *and ask it to make the magic stop."*

"Your Majesty, kill the butterfly and the magic will go."

However, despite the many opportunities for speaking and listening in English that these activities provided, they were largely undertaken on a monolingual basis and little or no use was made of the children's home languages. Where the project was more successful was in accommodating children's different cultural experiences.

Creative gaps

The project made extensive use of the idea of "creative gaps" that required the participants "to construct meaning actively through imaginative engagement" (Winston, 2003, p. 15).

These varied in the degrees of openness that they offered to the children. At one end of the continuum resided invitations to children to contribute from a limited pallet of responses. An example of this was in telling part of the Jack and the Beanstalk story; the practitioner would often pretend to lose the thread of her narrative and would ask the children to fill in her gaps with words of their own. Here, there was a sense of a restricted range of potential responses where it was possible for children to "get it wrong". A shift along the continuum and children were still being asked to contribute from a limited pallet but the sense of a right and wrong answer began to diminish. This was the case when the children were asked to make up some magic words in order to create the spell which would take away King Midas' golden touch. A step further along the continuum and the degree of openness increased, the pallet of potential responses was broader and the sense of right and wrong supplanted by the ability of the children to articulate a rationale for their contributions. As the structure around the activity decreased so the permission for children to bring more of themselves and their own experiences into the drama increased. This took place when the children were asked to decide what Little Red should pack in her basket to take to her grandmother's – a journey they were about to role play – they suggested chapattis, and mimed for the practitioner how to make them. Finally at the far end of the continuum was the opportunity for children to make up and play out their own stories.

As has been previously referred to, many of these stories bore the traits of the established stories that had gone before them, but some contained ingredients that suggested that children were drawing on and using their stories as a means of validating aspects of themselves and their own identity. One instance of this in action was when a small group of children in one setting developed a story featuring a journey on a magic carpet to Pakistan. They decided that part of the narrative took place in a shop and spontaneously began to role play, bartering with the facilitator in a mixture of their home language and English. The children responsible for creating this story were of Pakistani heritage and were evidently bringing to the story experiences that were familiar to them.

It appears, then, that the gaps offering the least structure and the greatest openness proved the most productive in yielding responses embodying a cultural dimension. However, working with such openness did not come without challenge – principally in relation to children's narrative expectations.

With stories that were known to them from their classrooms, such as Little Red Riding Hood and Jack and the Beanstalk, children used the familiar narrative structure as a means of navigation at times when they could not understand specific moments of interaction or when their English was insufficient to allow them to follow detailed moments of storytelling. Any attempts to deviate from what they understood to be the established story were consequently met with some resistance. However, in order to open up gaps for children's personalised responses, a deviation from the established form is exactly what was required. Similarly, when it came to the original story-making sessions, although the children reportedly enjoyed making up their own collective narrative, they also struggled with the task. Here the lack of a story-structure or an agreed universal theme meant that they had no frame of reference for contributing ideas and no means of contextualising their language usage. It was apparent that within the project there was a tension between the aspiration to accommodate children's own cultural experiences and their ability to respond to the opportunities provided.

Fine tuning the balance between providing structure and opening up spaces for children's responses, in particular those embodying aspects of their cultural experience, is an area of ongoing consideration for this work and although as yet untested, the following suggestions explore ways in which this balance might be more readily achieved:

- connecting more to classroom teaching to encourage the exploration of different versions of the same tale to allow children to see stories as fluid, changeable and ultimately something that they can influence;

- teasing out common characters and themes from the different versions and using these as a basis for drama sessions to provide children with a means of steering their way through areas of openness within the narrative;

- selecting stories that are less well known but that contain strong, universal underpinnings or familiar cultural elements to provide some recognisable structure, at the same time as leaving space for children to imprint something of themselves;

- including culturally relevant artefacts as a stimulus for generating original stories or selecting objects that point towards a particular "type" of story (quest, courtly, magical) to set up broad narrative parameters.

Small groups

One approach that was critical in realising the overarching aim of the project – to enable children to learn English through drama and story – was working with a small group. Learning as part of a whole class presents EAL children with considerable difficulties as it involves public risk-taking. Within such an environment EAL children often join in with the general consensus as a way of making less visible any deficiencies they have in speaking English; however, this also means that they may never have the opportunity to express and have valued their own original ideas, thoughts and questions.

Working in small groups offered a number of benefits to the project:

- It allowed the sessions to foster a culture of turn-taking, where every child got to have his or her say. Because the group was small in size the children were able to wait and listen while everyone had the chance to contribute. This also had the residual benefit of building social skills such as patience and respect for others.

- There was space for children to process the language that had been used or that they wanted to use. It was common for there to be a "satellite delay" between a question being posed in English and the child's reply. Small group work accommodated the wait necessary for children to think and formulate their responses.

- The small group dynamic meant that the children gained familiarity with one another quickly. This resulted in them talking more freely, taking greater risks with their suggestions and showing more initiative in posing questions than they reportedly did in class.

- Where children shared home languages, the small group allowed them to provide informal linguistic support to one another. This was most common during paired role play.

- Working with such small numbers of pupils meant that children's needs were more visible and could be easily identified and addressed. For example when a child could not understand a task due to his or her lack of English, time could be taken to reinforce, repeat or model the activity.

- The low numbers also allowed activities to be given "breathing space". Time could be allocated to planning and practising, for example deciding on what to say to a character in role and establishing appropriate vocabulary. Following the realisation of a task, children could also be given the space to reflect back, for example children supplying the thoughts and feelings for a character they have just role-played.

- Because of the small numbers involved, children got to see the very real impact of their ideas and interactions on the story itself. This increased their sense of ownership over the material which in turn increased their levels of commitment and motivation.

Perhaps the most interesting aspect of working with the children in a small group was the status it afforded them. Very often EAL children are categorised as having a special need, and operating in two or more languages is seen as a barrier to learning and not something worthy of celebration. Working as a part of a select group gave the children a different sense of their "special" status. Because the focus was placed on drama and story and not on learning English, the children returned to their classrooms as "experts" and would often take it upon themselves to show other children the things they had learned on the project, as the comments from this teaching assistant show:

> "Just wanted to share something lovely with you. [Child A] turned up with his story bag. This afternoon he sat in a big chair and showed the class all of its contents. His words 'it can be anything you want it to be'. He then chose the children and he encouraged them to take part in his story. He is going home to write it tonight as a thank you."

The way ahead?

The delivery of this project has taken The Play House part way on a journey and while the company is able to look back and reflect on some of the successes of the ride so far it still has some way to go in consolidating and building upon what it considers to be an area of emerging practice. The road ahead is signposted with further aspirations: to find more meaningful opportunities to integrate children's home-language talk, to co-deliver with bilingual teaching assistants, to involve older pupils working with younger children to translate their home-language stories into English, to introduce more culturally diverse stories into the repertoire and perhaps even to target children from shared language backgrounds to work together.

However, this road passes by a backdrop that at present remains monolingual. During the project there were many times when children were offered the opportunity to use their home languages with peers – to plan, role play, tell their stories and perform – but on nearly every occasion they did not take this offer up. The following quotation perhaps outlines the reason why and what the road ahead needs to look like to give children sufficient permission to speak in their home language as a means of also learning the English language.

> If children understand that their languages are regarded by the school as peripheral, those languages will remain silent. The occasional storytelling session in home language is not a genuine and full role for children's languages in their learning Children revert to English because they do not have a genuine choice of using their preferred language; the language of the school is English. We will only enable children to use their strongest or preferred language when we make those languages part of the legitimate learning medium of the classroom. This does not, of course require all teachers to speak all languages; it does require all teachers to provide opportunities for their use in the mainstream curriculum.
>
> (Blackledge, 1994, pp. 50–51)

This quotation is now nearly twenty years old but still holds true for many children and the classrooms in which they are being educated. Perhaps in the next twenty years the slow pace of change can be accelerated and this vision finally realised.

Acknowledgements

This chapter draws on the insights, anecdotes and evidence of the practitioners who developed the project with children and teachers. My thanks to Juliet Fry, Juliet Raynsford, Nicole Robey and Gillian Twaite.

References

Baker, C. (2002) *Foundations of Bilingual Education and Bilingualism* (3rd ed.). Clevedon: Multilingual matters.

Blackledge, A. (1994) *Teaching Bilingual Children*. Stoke on Trent: Trentham Books.

Blackledge, A., & Creese, A. (2010) *Multilingualism: A critical perspective*. London: Continuum Books.

Winston, J. (2003) *An Evaluation of Catalyst's "Changes"*. University of Warwick, Unpublished.

Winston, J. (2004) *Drama and English at the Heart of the Curriculum*. London: David Fulton.

4

Theatre, Language Learning and Identity (2)

Empowering Additional Language Learners through Classroom Drama Projects

Erene Palechorou and Joe Winston

This chapter makes an argument for the power of drama as a pedagogic tool for additional language learners. In particular, it focuses on the relationship between specific aspects of identity and additional language learning and identifies why and how drama pedagogy can respond to the pedagogic challenges this relationship presents. In order to illustrate this, we draw upon a drama project that took place in a Cypriot primary classroom where a high percentage of pupils were from different ethnic origins and spoke languages other than Greek at home. The main objective of this project was to examine how to use drama as a pedagogic method to facilitate the acquisition of Greek as an additional language by ethnic minority children in a mainstream Cypriot classroom.

Contextual information

In this primary school, a high percentage of the children came from different ethnic origins and faith communities. The specific drama project was conducted with a class of ten-year-old pupils in which six of the sixteen pupils, two boys and four girls, came from different ethnic backgrounds, and therefore had different home languages. What is more, their level of fluency in the Greek language varied according to the period of time they had been in Cyprus. More specifically, Alan and Elena from Lithuania, with Russian as their home language, had been living in Cyprus for three years and therefore their level of understanding, speaking and writing Greek was quite high. Maria from Bulgaria and Susan from Egypt, with Bulgarian and Arabic as their home languages respectively, had been living in Cyprus for almost two years and they were able to communicate in Greek, but not very fluently. Sara from Syria, who also had Arabic as her first language, and Orchan from Kurdistan, with Kurdish as his first language, had been in Cyprus not more than three months and their level of fluency was limited.

For any child, starting a new school can be a frightening experience. This can only be exacerbated by the added pressures of not understanding the language, becoming accustomed to a new lifestyle in a new country and at the same time, trying to retain one's own identity. In terms of language learning, this group of ethnic minority pupils faced the additional task of having to learn to communicate informally in the Cypriot idiom while being expected to acquire and use standard Greek in the formal environment of school. There are specific settings where speaking and writing standard Greek is demanded or considered polite, such as in the media, in the presence of non-Cypriot Greeks and in formal occurrences in school classrooms. The task of distinguishing which to use and when is difficult even for native speakers. Furthermore, although all Cypriots understand mainland Greeks, the Cypriot dialect varies greatly through local pronunciation and idiomatic structures. There are further levels of complexity here. Pupils with Greek as an Additional Language (GAL) need to maintain their first language as the language they speak at home, and as an integral part of their cultural heritage and identity, despite the fact that it is never used as the language of instruction in school. They are, in effect, not only learning a new language but also trying to contextualise all their other learning within this new language rather than in their own. This can be further hindered by the fact that classroom discussion ordinarily depends upon one social register, that of teacher–pupil exchange, in particular, the standard question–answer model.

It is unsurprising, then, that this group of GAL students often maintained a noticeable silence and their non-participation was interpreted, mostly by their classmates, as a lack of academic ability and a sign of weakness. Consequently they were often victims of bullying. It is worth mentioning, too, that even though some of the GAL pupils shared the same mother tongue, they rarely used it to communicate with each other in front of their Greek-Cypriot classmates for fear of censure or ridicule. This combination of anti-social behaviour and low self esteem was having an evident negative effect on their academic, emotional and social well being, especially in the case of the three girls, Maria, Susan and Sara, who were extremely shy and nervous. Their limited Greek-Cypriot vocabulary and low level of understanding effectively prevented them from joining existing friendship groups and attempts on their part had been rejected by the Greek-Cypriot pupils. As a reaction to this, one of the two GAL boys, Orchan, was beginning to display very challenging behaviour. He would leave the class at will, attack pupils and damage school property, anything to gain his classmates' or teachers' attention. Consequently, other children were unwilling to work with him.

The GAL pupils' problems were compounded by negative behaviour patterns demonstrated by the rest of the class and attributable to what are generally termed poor social skills. In particular, the class had real difficulties with group work; in listening to one another, co-operating, sharing ideas or putting the interests of the group before their own individual concerns. Any demonstration of weakness was seen as an opportunity to laugh at and mock the child in question and high levels of disruptive behaviour seriously impeded teaching and learning. Furthermore, boys and girls were unwilling to work together, and both sexes seemed to be engaged in a continuous, argumentative contest to gain power and status within the class.

Challenges and negotiating a drama contract

Before embarking upon the drama project, Erene was well aware of the risks and challenges facing her. The most significant of these was the fact that these children had never worked with drama before. In the Cypriot Educational System the closest terms to 'educational drama and theatre' are 'θεατρικό παιχνίδι' ('theatrical play') and 'θεατρική αγωγή' ('educational theatre'), which had not been, at the time, included as subjects in the National Curriculum. Consequently, most often the experiences children shared about 'drama' ('δράμα') or 'theatre' ('θέατρο') were limited to theatrical performances they had attended with the school. Drama as a form of creative teaching differed from the traditional instructional model that they were used to. Erene was naturally concerned with how children might respond to a new learning style that would require them to demonstrate the necessary physical self control that working in a drama space demands. In addition, how would they manage to work in groups, bearing in mind the lack of co-operation and respect for one another they normally demonstrated? Erene was encouraged by the positive and trusting relationship she had built with the children but nonetheless realised that a contract needed to be established in order to create a safe and positive learning environment. She therefore spent some time negotiating a small list of rules and behavioural objectives with the children before beginning the project. For each of these rules, the pupils were asked to agree upon a specially designed 'symbol' so that everyone in the class could understand them. This was significant for the GAL pupils, a small, initial step in creating an environment in which everyone's needs were to be taken into account, and in which all students would be respected and treated equally.

The initiation of the project and first impressions

The first few drama lessons seemed to confirm Erene's initial reservations. Behavioural problems did not diminish; on the contrary, they were magnified. One of the more constant and frustrating examples was the refusal of three strong-willed boys, including Orchan, to participate in some of the activities. Erene found herself constantly forced to return to the drama contract, but after a lot of discussion and practice, small changes in behaviour could be noted and, in particular, she was pleased to remark small but positive changes in the social behaviour and language ability of the GAL pupils, who were gradually participating more confidently, becoming more secure in their use of Greek and evidently beginning to enjoy themselves. After some weeks, Erene felt the need to sharpen the drama work so it could better serve the specific learning and social objectives she had identified.

The learning objectives of the drama scheme: 'The Missing Girl'

In rethinking her approach, Erene's aims were orientated around a range of broad concerns. She wished to improve the language learning of all the students while placing the needs of the GAL as central rather than peripheral to the project. These were inclusive of speaking, listening, reading and writing skills. However, what was of particular significance was the underpinning social learning and the aims here were varied and ambitious. She wished to increase the children's empathy and tolerance of 'difference'; encourage them to work equitably and positively together; to gain insight and appreciation of other languages and cultures; to improve social behaviour and their relationships with one another; to work creatively together by experimenting with ideas and solving problems. In addition, for the GAL students, she wanted to find a space for them to celebrate rather than hide their own cultural identities, in the belief that this would raise their self esteem. There is a danger, of course, that such a wish list might present drama as a magical formula to solve all pedagogical and social problems in one fell swoop. Erene was never this naïve. Nevertheless, the scheme as it unfurled exceeded her expectations; or rather the children's responses to it did. The following account describes how and examines why.

Description of the drama scheme

In attempting to plan a drama scheme with such ambitious aims, Erene knew that it would need to hold the children's interest over a long period of time. 'The Missing Girl' was taught over eight one-hour sessions and the story centered upon the ten-year-old missing daughter of a fictional Swedish ambassador whose family had been in Cyprus for the last six months. The children were asked to behave 'as if' they were experts in order to solve the mystery behind her disappearance and to co-operate with one another to solve what turned out to be a case of kidnapping. What made the story particularly interesting and powerful, especially for the GAL pupils, was the fact that the girl did not speak Greek, but several other languages, since she had lived in various countries due to her father's job. Although Erene had a planned structure for this scheme before beginning to teach it, the children's ideas directed the plot and made the story more fascinating and enjoyable for them. It was structured to include a range of strategies, which ensured that all children would be equally included and actively involved throughout. We will now describe these strategies and discuss the ways in which they were particularly empowering for the additional language learners.

Strategies for empowering additional language learners through drama

Selecting the drama material

A key to the success of the drama was the selection of the material. The central aims that guided this selection were as follows:

- The drama of 'The 'Missing Girl' included a lot of action and mystery, arousing curiosity and excitement, elements to capture the interest of most ten-year-old children.

- The drama provided a strong context for the children to practise listening, speaking, reading and writing.

- The drama placed GAL pupils in the centre of the action, since their knowledge of languages other than Greek was essential for the continuance of the drama.

Drama structures provide a powerful way of putting language into action as they give children the opportunity to become physically and linguistically part of the story by taking on the roles of the characters and imagining they are facing the same problems themselves. An exciting plot was seen as significant by Erene to help her confront dynamically the social conflicts in the class. She wanted to bring the students closer together as a group with the shared goal of solving a problematic situation. Furthermore, she hoped that the shared experiences inside this specific drama might unsettle some ingrained attitudes and gradually lead to a change in understanding. The scheme she devised was original but inspired by the drama 'Detectives', which is described in O'Neil and Lambert's book *Drama Structures* (1982). Below we explain how the plot and the drama activities progressed through the eight one-hour sessions.

First session

Erene began in role as the mother of the missing girl, asking for the children's co-operation and help to find her daughter, a student of their school. This introductory discussion established some basic facts about the story, in particular that the girl had gone missing the night before during a masque party at the Swedish embassy. The children exchanged ideas on possible ways to help find the girl, one of which was to create a poster, which meant that they had to ask the mother for specific information, such as what the girl had been wearing. In groups of three, they then organised, created and presented their poster to the class. What made this activity exciting and significant for the GAL pupils was the need to create it not only in Greek but also in their home languages since the girl didn't speak any Greek.

Second–third sessions

The next session opened with the children receiving a message through e-mail from the girl's mother thanking them for their help so far. However, because she was Swedish, it contained several spelling mistakes which the children identified and tried to correct. Erene then asked them to imagine themselves as TV-journalists and create an announce-ment for the TV-news. There was a brief discussion identifying similarities and differences between a poster and a TV-announcement after which Erene introduced herself as a particular friend of the girl's who could provide a deeper insight into her character: she was shy, didn't talk much, didn't have a lot of friends. The children in groups organised the TV-announcement, which was video-recorded. Everyone in each group had to say something in Greek and the GAL pupils could use their home languages as well. All TV-announcements were presented to the whole class and each group was asked to give positive feedback on the previous group's work.

Fourth session

Erene, now in role as a chief police officer, informed the children that the police had received information that the girl had been seen in a toy store. The children were asked to work in pairs, where 'A' was the police officer and 'B' the toy store owner. The police officer was to interrogate the toy store owner about what he or she had seen. These questions were rehearsed in advance. The children then shared the information they had gathered with the whole class group and it was then that they decided that the girl had, indeed, been kidnapped.

Fifth–sixth sessions

The children were now asked in three groups to imagine how the girl had been kid-napped and to create a detailed scenario for the whole class to re-enact in costume and masks that they had the chance to make themselves. There then followed three re-enactments, each involving the whole class. Erene narrated the early events of the night, which the class acted out through mime, whereupon a member from each of the groups in turn would take over and narrate their particular scenario for the kidnapping. In each case, a thought tracking strategy was used, giving members of the class the chance to speak out publicly what they imagined the thoughts, reactions or feelings of the girl to be.

Seventh session

The children now decided upon the scenario they preferred: that the kidnappers were Greek co-workers of the girl's father who were holding her for a ransom in an old house in a small town near the city but were treating her quite well. The children, in four groups, had to work out a plan for tricking the kidnappers. They knew it would be safer if they used languages other than Greek to communicate with the girl. Moreover, they knew their plan needed to avoid violence. Each group then shared their plan by acting it out.

Eighth session

When the girl had finally been rescued, Erene announced that she would be coming to the school. At this point Elena and Alan from Lithuania, who both have Russian as their home language, were asked to take on the roles of the missing girl and her translator respectively. Children could ask questions about her experience, her feelings and thoughts and, at the end, were asked to write a few words to make her feel safe and welcome after all she had been through.

Selecting the drama techniques and conventions

In seeking to use drama activities that would be inclusive, both culturally and linguistically, Erene found the **Mantle of the Expert** particularly useful. This strategy encourages students to behave 'as if' they are experts helping to solve a problematic situation associated with their expertise. In 'The Missing Girl', being addressed respectfully by the teacher had an immediate effect on children with different behavioural issues. The shy and quiet children were willing to participate and share their thoughts and opinions, the boys who normally misbehaved were interested enough to listen and ask pertinent questions; and for GAL pupils, fear of making mistakes in the target language ceased to be an issue. Instead, they would make strong efforts to talk in the authority register required by an 'expert'. For instance, during the fourth session Maria, in role as a police officer interrogating the toy store owner, not only tried to ask the questions in the target language but also tried to talk in the authority register which requires using the standard Greek language. This will be obvious to any Greek readers in the transcription below, where only a few of the words are in the Cypriot idiom.

> Κύριε Γιώργο, γεια σου, εγώ είμαι αστυνομικός και θέλω να σου κάμω ερωτήσεις ... Τι ώρα ήρτε κορίτσι στο κατάστημα σου; Το κορίτσι ήταν μόνο του; ... Μπορείς να μου πεις τι φορούσε παρακαλώ (Mr George, hello, I am a police officer and I would like to ask you some questions. What time did the girl come to the store? Was she alone? Could you please tell me what she was wearing?)

What is also significant in this specific example is that Maria understood what the activity required and managed to communicate effectively with her partner, even if there were several grammatical mistakes in her questions. She was further assisted by the fact that the kinds of question the police officer would ask had been rehearsed in advance.

The traditional relationship between teacher and pupils was changed in this strategy. Children formed and asked questions far more than they would in normal classroom activities and communicated them purposefully. Furthermore the strategy involved a lot of group work – creating posters, TV-messages and so on – and was structured to allow GAL and Greek-Cypriot children to mix. Observing the groups, Erene realised that GAL pupils were beginning to share their ideas and that these were being valued. Additionally, language was being used purposefully, as a tool for socialising, thinking, communicating and expressing ideas and emotions, as well as for forming actions. The aforementioned were identified in the first session, during the creation of the poster for the missing girl. Due to the fact that languages other than Greek were necessary for the creation of the poster, the GAL children were suddenly the centre of attention in each group, being called upon to translate ideas into their home languages. The Greek-Cypriot children were very interested in seeing something written in a language so different from their own and were continually asking the GAL students to read out loud what they had written. It was exciting to watch GAL children feeling proud of their home language as the key for moving the dramatic action forward.

Another particularly effective drama convention proved to be **teacher-in-role**. Erene took on three different roles as the drama progressed: the role of the mother of the missing girl in the first session, of one of her friends in the second and of a police officer in the fourth. Students were encouraged as investigators to question the mother and friend in order to gain additional clues to help find the girl and to discuss regularly with the police officer the progress of the investigation. The children's excitement on meeting a new character was demonstrative but the strategy was challenging for both teacher and pupils. The greatest challenge was to address all pupils' suggestions without making anyone feel afraid that they would be rejected or – worse – laughed at. What was particularly encouraging, however, was the way in which the children were noticeably trying out different language registers according to the person they were meeting. This approach also focused on the cultural differences that determine which registers and dialects the Greek-Cypriots consider appropriate to particular situations. In particular, it assisted GAL pupils in understanding that the use of the Cypriot dialect is more appropriate in informal situations, whereas the Greek language is to be used in formal interactions. For instance, during the second session, while video-recording the TV-announcement as a journalist, Susan, the little girl from Egypt, said in standard Greek: '*Το κορίτσι έχει ξανθά μαλλιά και αρέσει της να φορεί μια κόκκινη κορδέλα*' (The girl has blonde hair and likes to wear a red headband). If she had been using the Cypriot idiom she would have said '*Το κορίτσι έσιει ξανθά μαλλιά τζαι αρέσκει της να φορεί μια κόκκινη κορδέλα*'. In this example, we can see Susan's effort not to use the Cypriot idiom. She doesn't succeed in it completely, since the correct phrase in standard Greek would be '*Το κορίτσι έχει ξανθά μαλλιά και της αρέσει να φορά μια κόκκινη κορδέλα*'. However, what is significant here is that Susan seems to understand that the 'real-life' situation she finds herself in necessitates talking in the authority register, as well as changing from the Cypriot idiom to standard Greek. In a subsequent interview, when asked why she had used standard Greek, she said '*Γιατί ήμουν στην τηλεόραση*' (Because I was on TV).

Another convention that assisted GAL pupils in particular was **narrated action**, in which the teacher narrates a part of the story while the class acts it out though mime. Volunteers or selected pupils have to show physically everything that the teacher narrates, even objects, and improvise the dialogue between the characters. This strategy was used to re-enact the night of the kidnapping and particularly supported the speaking and listening skills of the GAL pupils. By actively taking on the roles of the characters in the story, children had to listen carefully to the narrator in order to identify when they had to talk and what they had to say and then repeat or improvise the words of the character. The repetition of phrases enabled all children, regardless of their fluency in the additional language, to feel confident and safe as they spoke. It is worth mentioning that the night of the kidnapping was enacted three times, from three different points of view, leading to different scenarios based on the ideas of the children and providing them with the opportunity to see that different people see things differently, taking them one step forward in accepting points of view different from their own. As Alan said during his interview:

> I really liked doing three times the night of the masque party. I liked all of them but most of all the one that group C did. Ours had more action, but their idea was really funny, we laughed a lot.

In order to tackle anti-social behaviour, Erene found **thought tracking** to be a useful strategy. In one example, the action was frozen during a scene where a child was in role as the missing girl. The participants touched the girl, who spoke out loud her private thoughts, reactions or feelings. After experiencing her story for themselves, the children could begin to empathise with her experience of being in a new country and unable to speak the language. This obviously and deliberately paralleled the recent experience of the GAL students, which was now the centre of attention and interest. The GAL students were experts as they, in particular, understood how she felt. The boy from Kurdistan, Orchan, whose level of fluency in Greek was extremely low, appeared to participate only physically in most of the activities, but in this particular activity he was very eager to touch the girl and say words or small phrases such as, 'όχι φίλους' (no friends), 'Θυ ω ένο' (I am upset). Erene was impressed by Orchan's efforts, but what was most interesting was the fact that his classmates did not make fun of his grammatical mistakes as they usually did. Instead, they accepted the thoughts and feelings as though they understood they were his own as well as the girl's.

Creating a physical context for experiencing language

A key pedagogical advantage of drama for additional language learners lies in its multi-modal character. Drama does not depend on language alone, but uses objects, gestures, sounds and images along with words in order to communicate meaning. Children therefore have the opportunity to draw and create meaning not only from the spoken language, but also from the physical context and the visual and aural signals in which it is embodied.

Erene opened this scheme with a visual image created from some personal objects, including a book of fairytales and a teddy-bear that belonged to the little girl. These visual clues captured the children's attention and helped them identify the main character of the story. As there were no words involved, GAL students were equally able to draw meaning from these objects.

Many of the drama strategies, such as narrated action, engaged children in using their body language to express thoughts and ideas, creating a non-threatening environment for GAL pupils, in which participation was not dependent solely upon linguistic skill. In being released from the constraints of language, additional language learners could express their thoughts through their bodies and not solely in a language they were uncomfortable with. Most importantly, this physicality, different from traditional classroom activity, provided them with a simple way to join in, developing their confidence through gestures, posture and movement rather than through an insistence that they use the target language. At the same time, the other children were given the opportunity to see that even if GAL pupils are less able to speak, read or write Greek they could still participate in physically striking ways. And if at first the GAL students did not entirely understand the activity, they had the opportunity to watch and listen to others and decide when and how they would participate. For instance, during the seventh session, when the groups were working out a plan for tricking the kid-nappers, Maria got to be in role as one of them. This role was in contrast with her own personality and at first she did not want to participate. Maria was a shy and generally low profile girl, always needing a lot of encouragement. Nevertheless, while rehearsing their plan, her group really tried to encourage her by saying 'Come on Maria, we need you to do this, we cannot have just one kidnapper, just try.' What is more, they were showing her how to become a mean kidnapper by using her body and face. At her own pace, she joined in and by the time they presented their plan to the class she seemed an entirely different person. Her facial expressions, as well as her body language, made her a very convincing villain! What was most important, though, was her response to this experience:

> I didn't want to be the kidnapper but the other children showed me how to do it and told me what I could say. I was trying to do an angry and mean face but it was hard because we were laughing a lot. I liked that activity, it was fun.

Gradually, because most of the activities were whole-group, by giving and taking ideas from one another, GAL pupils gained in confidence and it was exhilarating to watch other children supporting them throughout.

Through the physical context created in drama, the GAL children were able to con-nect the oral language of the story with the physical language of their actions, developing specific pieces of vocabulary and sentence structures. An example of this kind of language development could be seen in Sara, who had limited vocabulary and fluency in the Greek language. In the thought tracking activity at the end of the seventh session, Sara showed that she had picked up an impressive amount of vocabulary. She used the words 'μόνη' (lonely), 'φοβάμαι' (I am scared) and small sentences such as 'Είμαι δυστυχισμένη' (I am unhappy), 'Θέλω να κάνω φίλους' (I need friends). I believe this was because during the drama sessions she was given the opportunity to understand these new words and phrases through experience, as well as pick up additional clues from the gestures and expressions, the tone and atmosphere that was created in the specific drama situation. Furthermore, she was given the chance to express these feelings in a 'real-life' situation.

Creating a context that reflects the cultural and linguistic diversity of the classroom

If teachers and students ignore the cultural and linguistic diversity of their classrooms, the impact on GAL students is likely to be a negative one. If, however, the teacher can find a context for valuing the mother tongues of these students within the curriculum then the learning experience for all pupils can be rewarding.

Throughout the drama of 'The Missing Girl' Erene attempted to include the different mother tongues of the GAL children within the story. The context she established from the outset immediately raised the status of the non-Greek languages in the classroom and consequently that of the pupils who spoke them. The Greek-Cypriot children quickly realised and appreciated that the GAL children were a vital resource to help solve the mystery. Often groups needed at least one GAL pupil as a member in order to complete the set task – to write the text of the poster or record the TV-message, for example. The children first had to discuss the content of the poster and of the message, and the linguistic and social benefits from these activities for all the children and particularly for the GAL pupils were multiple. In terms of social learning, Erene was particularly struck by the ways in which they negotiated and reached compromises, as the following brief example illustrates.

In her group, Elena from Lithuania took a leading role, since she felt powerful enough as the only one who spoke a language other than Greek and soon assigned all the members of the group different tasks, such as drawing a picture or writing the script. Before writing in Russian the group discussed what the message on the poster should include and what other information should support it, such as a contact number. Surprisingly, there was no squabbling and the children in the group co-operated effectively and presented an impressive piece of work. During the presentation of the poster all members, including the non-Russian speakers, were able to say what was written in the Russian language. GAL pupils were taking on responsibility for the learning, leading the group work and taking decisions, gaining a high status position inside the group and feeling proud of their cultural identities. This activity, more than any other, led to a significant improvement in their confidence and self-esteem, as they saw their mother language as a benefit rather than a drawback; at the same time, it encouraged the development of their target language skills. Their voices were being heard and they were showing the class that they had a lot to offer. Most importantly, the Greek-Cypriot students were so excited by the experience of listening to and writing a different language that they were continually asking the GAL pupils to teach them new words and phrases from their languages. Such can be the power of a well chosen dramatic story.

The different languages of the GAL pupils were the key to the drama in other activities, too; when children were given the opportunity to talk to Alan and Elena as the girl and her interpreter, for example, to find out what she had endured. The questions were discussed before the activity and the fairytale that belonged to the little girl, written in Arabic, was read out loud to the class by Susan. This was Cinderella, and the class was excited to find out that children from different countries shared the same stories. During the reading, Susan stopped and showed the pictures to the children and they identified similarities and differences between the versions they knew. They were astonished to learn that the convention of reading left to right is not common to all languages and the book, now an object of fascination rather than something merely foreign and strange, led the Cypriot children to reflect upon what they shared in common with the GAL students, as well as what marked them out as different. As Andrew, a Greek-Cypriot pupil commented:

Μπορεί να μην έχουμε μόνο τα ίδια παραμύθια αλλά και παρόμοια παιχνίδια ή άλλα πράγματα. (Maybe we do not only have the same fairytales but very similar games, or other stuff as well).

Reflecting after the drama

Reflecting on the drama can be an effective way for all students to become actively involved in their own learning. Erene considered it necessary to give children the opportunities and strategies to assess themselves and each other in order to understand how they might improve. With this in mind, after the presentation of all the TV-announcements in the third session, each group was asked to reflect and critically comment on the work of the former presenting group, based on criteria that had been discussed in advance, such as the language register, atmosphere and tone. The class also rehearsed how to make constructive comments without hurting people's feelings. This was important for protecting not only GAL but all pupils from negative criticism. The results were very satisfying and students' comments were accurate. The process had a positive effect on John, for example, a very smart Greek-Cypriot boy, who often made harsh comments to his classmates, especially to GAL pupils, whenever they made mistakes. He commented:

> *This presentation was very good. The language they used was the appropriate one. I liked it that they had a serious facial expression. In my opinion the presentation will improve if they add more details about the girl's appearance.*

During this activity, and throughout the drama as a whole, Erene's role as the sole provider of knowledge was diminished. Instead, she became an '*εμψυχωτή*' (encourager) as children became more responsible for their own learning and for sharing their knowledge.

Erene was careful throughout to assess the level to which her linguistic and social objectives were succeeding and to identify any issues that needed re-addressing. She was able to observe significant progress in the language work of GAL children, especially in their acquisition of new vocabulary, in pronunciation and in sentence formation. She believes that much of this progress was due to the inclusion of the different mother tongues as this gave them the opportunity first of all to contextualise new learning in their home languages, rather than in the target language. The fictional context provided many authentic opportunities for the development of speaking, listening, reading and writing. For instance, the writing activity in the eighth session was derived from the drama the children had just experienced, and this made it not only purposeful, but even fun and exciting. When they were asked to write a few words they would say to the little girl to make her feel safe and welcome after all she had been through, Alan from Russia wrote:

> *Μη φοβά'σε. Εγω' θα ι'με φι'λος σου. Αν θε'λης εγω' να μιλο' σου Ρω'σικα για να καταλαβε'νης. Εγω' μα'θω σου κε ελληνικα'. Εντα'ξη* (Don't be scared, I will be your friend. If you like I will speak to you in Russian so you can understand. I will teach you Greek as well. OK?).

What is impressive here in Alan's written work is that, despite his spelling and syntactic mistakes, the content is meaningful and communicates successfully what he wants to say, something he was not always able to do. In his written work he proudly refers to his home language and is not hesitant to use it in front of others as he had been in the past. The home languages of the GAL students were used so often inside the drama that they ceased to be strange to any of the children. This was shown in John's written comment:

> *Μη στεναχωριε'σαι που δε μιλα'ς ελληνικα'. Πολλα' παιδια' στο σχολει'ο μας ε'ρχονται απο' α'λλες χω'ρες και δε μιλου'ν ελληνικα'...αν θε'λεις θα γι'νω εγω' φι'λος σου. Θα σου μα'θω κα'ποια παιχνι'δια που παι'ζουμε. Μπορει' να τα παι'ζετε και στη Σουηδι'α. Μπορει'ς να μου μα'θεις και εσυ'παιχνι'δια που παι'ζετε στη*

Σουηδία. (Don't be sad that you don't speak Greek. Many children in our school come from different countries and don't speak Greek ... so if you like I can be your friend. I can show you some games we play. Maybe you have the same in Sweden. And you can teach me some Swedish games).

John, a child who had constantly been dismissive of GAL pupils, was beginning to take their feelings into consideration in his writing.

In terms of social learning, Erene was able to witness on several occasions the children working together constructively and at the same time enjoying each other's company. She observed during their group work that they managed on the whole to put the interests of the group before their own individual concerns, valuing what others had to say and behaving appropriately. Impressive progress was made by Orchan, who, even if he was still participating sporadically, had at least stopped leaving the classroom. Now that he was being given the opportunity to be at the centre of attention for constructive reasons, he did not have to seek attention in negative ways and this led to him becoming gradually more accepted by the class. And physical participation in drama suited him. When asked 'What did you like most about the drama?' he answered:

Μου αρέσει παιχνίδια τζαι που δεν είμαι στο θρανίο, μου αρέσει εγώ κάμνω τον κακό απαγωγέα. (I like the games and that I am not sitting behind the desk, I liked that I was the bad kidnapper)

Conclusion

In this chapter, we have identified the ways that classroom drama can help additional language learners by focusing on their social and cultural needs as well as targeting their language learning. The GAL children needed to feel accepted, safe and relaxed inside their new cultural environment, as exemplified by the words of Susan and Maria:

Αρέσκει μου θέατρο γιατί εν κάμνω λάθη. (I like doing drama because I don't do any mistakes) *Το διάλειμμα παίζω με ούλλες κορούες παιχνίθκια που κάμαμε στο θέατρο.* (During break-time I play games that we did in drama with all the girls).

The results of this work exceeded our expectations but we want to emphasise that success did not appear overnight. It took almost twenty weeks of drama work and a lot of effort, especially from the children, but Erene was more than satisfied to see these changes persist after the conclusion of a project that had fostered a community of learners able to work together and enjoy each other's company. The children had, indeed, become more open and friendly with one another, not only inside the drama but also during break-time. It is not our intention, however, to pretend that all the class's social problems had been resolved. Important issues remained, such as poor gender relations, and these, too, needed to be addressed in a subsequent drama project. But that, as they say, is another story.

Reference

O'Neill, C., & Lambert, A. (1982). *Drama Structures*. London: Hutchinson.

5

Drama and Languages Education

Authentic Assessment through Process Drama

Julia Rothwell

In this chapter I explore the ways process drama can enrich and enliven the assessment regime of a middle school beginner language programme. The chapter draws on five months' language teaching which I did to collect data during my doctoral research. I taught a secondary co-educational class of twelve to thirteen year olds (first year secondary school) for their German lessons while the teacher who had invited me in observed the lessons. Throughout the project there was an emphasis on student participation through questionnaire, discussion and interview.

In the first part of the chapter I make links between assessment for learning and intercultural language learning and explain how I am using the term "authentic" to describe language assessment experiences. Following this I review the sequence of assessment tasks used in the unit of work to discuss how a process drama pedagogy provided opportunities for assessment tasks which encourage authentic communication skills in all learners. I explore how and why they can develop learners' confidence and capacity to interact spontaneously and how they can enhance the intercultural literacy of learners.

Assessment is arguably the most powerful force in most school programmes. Failure or low grades at assessment time can affect learners' long term attitude to the subject and their overall self esteem. Research over the last twenty years in both Australia and the UK recognises this fact (Black & Wiliam, 1998; Wyatt-Smith & Cumming, 2009; Alexander, 2010) Skilful design of assessment experiences which meet the systemic requirements *and* stimulate learners through connection to life beyond the school are crucial to retaining learners in language classrooms.

Assessment of languages

Scarino and Gould-Drakely (2009) claim that "Assessment has the power to influence what language is"; if the assessment is based on decontextualised grammatical accuracy then this is what learners will aim for, often to the detriment of their ability to take risks and negotiate meaning in a range of relationships and situations. Conversely, if assessment tasks are designed to assess the learner's capacity to *manipulate* the language they have learnt, to think about and *choose* language for specific situations and relationships, and to experiment with what they know about their own and other languages and cultures, then it is more likely they will be able to actually use language as a rich tool for engaging confidently and meaningfully with different communities at home and abroad.

Authentic language assessment tasks

Typically early level oral language assessment will focus on prepared language. Tasks such as role plays with palm cards and presentations with a Powerpoint are very common. Written assessment will often involve such activities as comprehension questions, grammar activities and cloze activities, albeit often disguised as games. There is of course a place for these activities, but I am suggesting that they are incomplete as assessment tasks because they do not represent authentic language in use. The word "authentic" has been widely used in an assessment context and can describe both language assessment tasks and effective assessment in general. For the purposes of this chapter, I use "authentic" to encompass three characteristics of effective communication.

First, it is partially *unrehearsed*. To prepare learners well for real life communication they need practice in spontaneous use of language, in making meaning with what little they have. Second, authenticity requires language *specific to the topic, relationship and mode* of the communication. Language is used differently depending on who is interacting with whom and why. The mode we use, oral or written, also affects our choice of language, and digital communication can require further modification. We also use bodies and faces to communicate alongside language, and this needs to be an integral part of an authentic language programme.

Finally, all these conditions of use are affected by the *culture in which the language sits*; text formats, language choices, accompanying gestures all vary according to culture, time and place. Without recognition that both our first and any additional languages are bound up with cultural beliefs, behaviours and histories, language remains sterile. In developing the assessment tasks for this process drama I have used these elements of authenticity to guide the design.

Assessment for learning

Scarino and Gould-Drakely (2009) suggest that the process of assessing this kind of active intercultural language learning involves both moment *in* time assessment and ongoing assessment *over* time. This kind of cumulative approach to assessment sits very neatly inside the assessment for learning model promoted by the New London Reform Group (Black & Wiliam, 1998) and re-advocated in the more recent UK Cambridge curriculum review

(Alexander, 2010). This assessment model involves not just point in time "summative" tests, but also informing students and teachers about student learning through assessment modes such as anecdotal evidence gathering, self and peer assessment and collected portfolios of work. As Black and Wiliam explain, assessment for learning lifts standards of achievement for all and lessens the gap between the stronger and weaker learners. This is particularly important in a class with a wide range of prior learning and language skills. Black and Wiliam's review shows that an ongoing teacher–student "conversation", with frequent feedback and encouragement, means learners become more willing to take risks, ask questions and rise to a challenge. Student responses to the tasks described below suggest that assessment for learning through drama can achieve these effects in the language classroom.

Languages assessment through process drama

So how can process drama help with all this? As we have seen in earlier chapters, drama provides ideal conditions for authentic language learning. Indeed, the assessment tasks embedded in this drama have an authenticity and immediacy which can be hard to achieve through more traditional tasks and tests. Enrolment of learners as fictional characters in an evolving narrative means they can experience a huge range of interaction types as the drama unfolds. The collaborative nature of the storying combined with the shift in interactional relationships (e.g. through the teacher also performing a role) means learners are more active and more equal partners in many of the learning experiences. Finally, a process drama encompasses reflective strategies which develop learners' understanding of the connections between language and culture. The rich context which process drama provides for all aspects of language learning also enhances opportunities for assessment of authentic language use.

Review of assessment tasks

The dramatic context for assessment

For this process drama the social question behind the drama was "What is it like to leave your home country forever, to live in a new land using a new language?" Our orientating pre-text was a picture from Shaun Tan's *The Arrival* (2007). I had become familiar with this book through work I did with early childhood pre-service teachers and was excited by the layers of meaning and imaginary worlds which the illustrations evoked. The picture of a man and woman standing by a suitcase in the kitchen stimulated both description of the scene in the target language and talk in English about leaving one's home. After pondering together what they could see in the picture and what might be in the suitcase, students were led into a migration scenario by choosing new identities from an authentic ship's list (found in the local library). The ship, *Sophie*, brought migrants from Hamburg to Brisbane in 1863. In role as the Australian descendants of these families at an unspecified date, the students were forced to leave Australia because of their German names and travel to Germany to live. They maintained this family grouping for much of the unit of work. To be accepted into their new land they had to prove they could speak the German language and, once landed, they had to adjust to the new language and culture around them while building a new everyday life.

Below I discuss the assessment task sequence from the process drama, *Sophie*. In keeping with the principles of assessment for learning, no task is regarded as a wholly discrete entity and is therefore discussed alongside the preparatory scaffolding activities which enrich it.

Task 1 Preparation

Life on board the *Sophie*:

Match captions to freeze frame photos in album to send home
Respond to signs and notices on board ship

Assessment format:

Individual work done at desk without collaboration

Scaffolding activities:

From a picture of people on deck in *The Arrival* choose which is you and sculpt your own body to match – so class as a whole re-creates picture. Ask class how each person seems to feel.

Freeze frame family group on ship

Shoulder tap asking how feel

Fill in speech bubbles for family member/s in photo (draft, feedback, repeat)

Task 1: Cartoon speech bubble, photograph album and reading ship's signs

This is an early assessment opportunity which combines several skills and modes of communication in its preparation. As can be seen in the preparation details above, the task moves from kinaesthetic to oral to written work, a sequence which mirrors the first language learning model, and the kinaesthetic element is very much a dramatic contribution. This combination of modes alerts learners to the idea that, in any culture, there are many modes of communication, and both the context and the mode are affected by the local situation.

The lead-up to the task involved freeze frames. For students learning to use a second language they are a succinct and popular "way in" to new settings, events and relationships and the associated vocabulary; they help draw beginners into the sensual and emotional element of the drama when words are lacking; they also provide a stimulus for intercultural discussion in terms of pragmatics, gesture and facial expression; and help to retain the sense of enrolment even when the work is purely language focused. These freeze frames provided me with an unanticipated assessment resource which enriched the unit throughout: I photographed the frames then used the photographs as resources. Initially I added a speech bubble to a family photograph for students to show someone's thoughts as he/she sat on deck. This served several purposes: it allowed for responses at many language levels; it connected the embodiment of the family's feelings in the photograph to language; it maintained a sense of role and therefore authenticity; it made a confidence-building, simple connection from oral work (e.g. shoulder tap, gossip mill on deck) to a form of "written speech"; I was able to provide individual feedback and to adapt planning accordingly. Students then did a second, unassisted speech bubble which I assessed for the record and which consolidated language they would need for the later reading task.

For the reading tasks I used more photographs (see Appendix). The paper test format of this assessment was a response to the observing teacher's request for a traditional point in time assessment to provide a recorded grade. Black and Wiliam (1998) suggest that "conditions under which formal tests are taken threaten validity because they are quite unlike those of everyday performance" (p. 9). As a compromise, although I devised paper based reading tasks as tests, the dramatic context authenticated the text. "Real" reading always has a purpose and authentic reading tasks should reflect this fact: first, students were asked to match their family photographs to captions for an album which friends back home would welcome. In the second task, as the students now "lived" half their class time on a ship, responding to ship's signs was meaningful. The ship's signs were in German but to cater for the beginners, questions about the signs were in English (see Appendix, Question B).

Responding to ship's signs (original signs in German, instructions in English)

1.   What would you do and why?

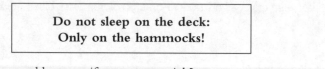

2.   Where would you go if you were seasick?

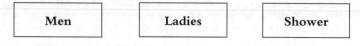

3.   When would you go and read on the deck?

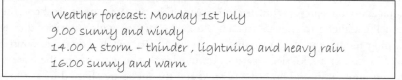

The signs were constructed from vocabulary which students had been exposed to but not in this form or context. Some students answered in German and some in English. I was happy with this at this early stage and looked just for a response which was either correct or well justified; authentic reading in this case consisted of knowing how to behave – not translating every word. Despite being short and simple, the task offered a limited opportunity to use more language and, as can be seen in the following response, to imagine oneself still in role.

In response to number 2, "Where would you go if you were seasick?" (men's, ladies' or shower room) one beginner student wrote:

"der Manner, denn ich bin der Vater." [the Men's, because I am the father.]

Not only does the student give a reason when he could have contented himself with a simple "Manner", he also remains in role to answer and uses a conjunction (because) to write a compound response in the target language. It is unusual to use this grammatical form so early in the programme, but this student was motivated to extend his language in role.

Task 2 Hot seat the captain after the storm. Undertake immigration interview

2A HOT SEAT (TEACHER IN ROLE)

This oral task sequence was designed to encourage different aspects of interaction. As the video data shows (extract below), the hot seat was an excellent medium for stimulating certain kinds of learners to stretch their language limits, and for encouraging listening skills and spontaneous response of various kinds. The immigration interviews, on the other hand, were a point in time assessment of specific language knowledge and use by all students. There is limited space here to discuss both tasks in detail, and my focus is on the hot seat as the task most removed from traditional language assessment.

Task 2a Preparation

Storm at Sea: Mutiny via hot seat Students listen to stories of storm at sea. Remonstrate with the Captain about lack of food and water for children (he doesn't speak English)

Assessment format:

Hot seat

Scaffolding activities:

Teacher and students develop a class soundscape of stormy weather to learn/revisit language describing weather

Student family groups brainstorm consequences of storm and create relevant freeze frame.

Teacher sequences photos of frames and tells story of storm using projected images of man and food overboard.

List of possible protest slogans and questions provided and drilled

Angry passengers confront Captain (teacher in role) and demand to know what he will do about situation using phrases provided and personal language

Class reflects on how the activity went

As an assessment task the hot seat provides for anecdotal assessment; evidence cannot be collected from all students because some will participate more actively/verbally than others – as in any protest meeting; ironically, the very authenticity of the interaction makes it unsuitable as point in time assessment of all students. I had limited experience of adopting a dramatic role in class (teacher-in-role) and embarked on this task with much trepidation. However, I was determined to try it because the drama needed intensifying and, as an assessment task, it richly reflected two of my criteria for authenticity: unrehearsed interaction *and language suited to a specific social relationship and purpose*.

The transcript below of a section of the exchange illustrates the efficacy of this process drama strategy for stimulating creative use of limited language in a very specific cultural context – an oral complaint between speakers with unequal power. Using German to make themselves understood only increased the unequal power relations for the students in role; they were now on the back foot as passengers versus the Captain, as students versus the teacher *and* as beginner speakers versus a native speaker. Not only were they enrolled as passengers complaining about the loss of food in a storm, they now also had genuine feelings of frustration brought on by their language limitations. Challenged in role and challenged as students, many responded spontaneously using language specific to the topic, relationship and mode.

Moreover, the enrolment of both teacher and students gave students the right to initiate conversation, even to argue with and accuse the teacher-as-captain, thus extending their capacity to sustain an interaction by appropriate questioning – a capacity Byram (1997, p. 99) argues is part of intercultural literacy. This kind of learner control over an interaction is rare in beginner language classrooms, including mine, but is a well documented benefit of using teacher-in-role in the drama field (e.g. O'Toole, 1992). The scene began with students all shouting a protest phrase, chosen from the whiteboard, as the captain entered. Then they mostly used their own words. Unfortunately the transcript cannot convey the energy and focus of all students which is apparent in the video

Hot seat transcript

original is all in German; unless otherwise indicated the German was accurate.

■ *// indicates overlap with next speaker*

St 1:	(chant style) We are hungry! //
Teacher/	
Researcher (T/R):	The containers all tipped over
St 1:	We are hungry!
St 20:	My children will go hungry. [Picking up on use of future tense from *different* phrase on whiteboard]
T/R:	The children will be ok …
St 1:	My child is dead (brief laughter).
T/R:	Your child is dead? Where is he? (St 2 points to St 5). He doesn't seem dead.
St 2:	I'm sick.
T/R:	You're sick. Good, then when we arrive in Germany you can have some medicine.
★★★St 18:	[using phrase off whiteboard at appropriate moment] What are you having to eat, Captain?
T/R:	Me?
St 18:	Yes.
T/R:	I'm eating nothing. I've had a bit of bread, nothing else. A bit of bread.
St 20:	Can't you see? [Kann du nicht sehe?]
T/R:	Se …What? What? See what?
St X:	St … storm [reference to cause of the food loss]
St 20:	(moves hands emphatically) There is no food! [Da keine Essen]
T/R:	There is a bit of food. You're all getting //
St 20:	So? //
T/R:	… water. //
St 20:	So? So?
T/R:	You're all getting water.
St 20:	No food.

T/R:	Lots of water [other st starts to mutter]
St 20:	The water's brown!
T/R:	The water is??
St 20 + St X:	Brown! //
St 1:	I am angry!

(Classroom video G, 2009)

At this point (★★★) there could have been a natural end to the conversation but a student kept the scene going by using a phrase from the whiteboard appropriately to move us on. This happens again after this extract when a low proficiency student rescues the limping conversation with an appropriate German phrase from the board "What a catastrophe!" On both occasions students have initiated a new topic to maintain interaction, a sophisticated skill in absolute beginners and something hard to generate in conventional assessment tasks. It is likely the playful nature of the dramatic enrolment is spurring them on.

The dramatic context was an important motivator in another way. I suggested students use German and move to English when necessary, but they only used German. When asked why, one student replied "The Captain doesn't speak English" and, indeed, this was a condition I had set at the start of the unit. It seems that the enrolment and storying encourages learners to rise to the challenge of making meaning in another language, even when not for point-in-time assessment.

2B IMMIGRATION INTERVIEWS

Task 2b

Immigration interviews: Language as gatekeeper

Only using German in interview will guarantee entry

Assessment format:

Interview in role as member of migrant family.
Teacher and other students in role as immigration officers.

Scaffolding activities:

Discussion of the need, or not, to speak the local language as you enter a country
Consolidation of self description language through board game and inside-outside circle Q and A.

Family groups interviewed in German to check that whole family can speak German; some questions are not prepared. Teacher in role as immigration officer; some students take turns to join her

One family smuggles stowaway in and covers for her at interview

For the later immigration interview task, students in role as migrants had to answer questions from the immigration officers about their personal details in order to disembark. Questions about personal details had been prepared for but as part of the drama extra questions were also asked. The work in the hot seat task had prepared students for this unpredictable element of the interview. The resulting intermittent spontaneity was a characteristic that differentiated these assessment interviews from the school's usual first oral assessment of a prepared self-introduction presented to the class. Several students commented that assessment tasks in role were more motivating than previous language assessment experiences. Comments included:

St 4: Like it was more exciting, like. When you're writing on a piece of paper, sometimes it's like really boring ... all the time ... But, you know, when you're doing stuff, it's better.

St 18: Putting yourself into the mood of it and ...

T/R: Yeah.

St 18: And, em, actually *doing* something ...

St 10: Yeah, you actually do something so instead of just sitting there and writing, you're actually ... you're actually acting it out, so you ...

Assessment through the drama was also meaningful to students in terms of authenticity:

St 2: I guess it was kind of like everyone wasn't laughing their heads off and stuff. It was more serious.

T/R: Okay. So the serious element of it?

St 2: Yeah, kind of made it feel more realistic, I guess.

Task 3: Written job application in Berlin

Task 3 Preparation

Applying for work

A written job application for a specific, chosen jub on a form provided.

Assessment format:

Written application done individually in quiet class after feedback on draft.

Scaffolding activities:

Discussion in L1 about possible reception in country and possible reasons

Mixed reception as pass through conscience alley and disembark down gangplank

Lone student in role goes round circle asking for work; students in role as employers choose individual response

Students in role given job list by migrant hostel warden. Discuss skills needed.

Choose jobs which can do without high level language

Freeze frame jobs and match photos to necessary skills Crossword puzzle in TL (clues also) for job types

Discuss generic desirable skills/personality traits. Create persuasive sentences about self

Sheet of questions relevant to job application for students to prepare; give feedback

Write application in class using headings on application form for guidance

Students had experienced informal and formal conversations; now I wanted a transition into formal written skills. I wanted a task which enriched and was enriched by the socio-cultural context and which both consolidated work in earlier tasks and regenerated recently acquired language. I also wanted an assessment text which gave all learners an opportunity to demonstrate text specific communicative skills.

A crucial element of the task, however, was its connection, via the drama, to events which have left huge traces in the socio-cultural life and language of Germany today. Nowadays tensions associated with the arrival and assimilation – or otherwise – of migrants are ongoing facts of both German and Australian social life, and language is one of the potential barriers to co-existence. We discussed first how local people might variously respond to the migrants and why. I then used an adaptation of the *conscience alley* technique whereby the family ran the gauntlet of both welcoming and antagonistic groups of local residents as they disembarked. As the pre-text for term 2 they then watched an edited selection of YouTube clips (in English) describing divided post-war Berlin.

The students were now in role in a hostel in Berlin in 1961, the year the Berlin Wall went up, and they have to find work. Connections to the drama's underlying social issues were again made since the initial job-choosing made space to talk, in English, about the jobs poor local language skills preclude in any society. In terms of cultural authenticity the draft application provoked feedback about choosing language appropriate for that text, in that culture, at that time, for that purpose. Resisting the "All I know" urge is the beginning of learning that topic, relationship and mode affect language choice. Several students confirmed that the immersion in the historical drama deepened their interest in the assessment tasks, for example:

> **St 20:** Well, it's easier to get German to come to you, like to speak and do German if you imagine yourself in a German environment.
>
> **St 18:** Exactly.

One student commented that the work was stimulating and he also made connections to the recent arrival of a boat of refugees in Australian waters

> **St 6:** Yeah, like the videos and then I saw there was like the news. It was like on that as well.
>
> **T/R:** Why did you like the videos?
>
> **St 6:** It like explained things about it.
>
> **T/R:** Okay, it explained things about … what?
>
> **St 6:** The Berlin Wall and why it was put up and everything.
>
> **T/R:** Okay. So why … it was in English, it was history. Why do you think it was interesting to you in a German lesson? …
>
> **St 6:** Because it helps you think.
>
> (Student Interviews 3, 4, 2009)

In a further example of cross-cultural connections another student clearly describes the effect of not only the adoption of a role, but of how that role changes as the drama progresses.

St 5: I think because when we were in the families, we had a person to be, but then when we did the migration, you had to be someone else because you couldn't be what you were before you migrated. You had to be something else. You couldn't speak like you normally would, or couldn't really act because the people where you were moving to thought differently of what you should be doing and not ...

(Student Interview 4, 2009)

In her final comment this student provides an unusually mature description of the possibility for misunderstandings arising from different world views. Not many students were so articulate, but in other ways, too, the open-ended process catered for diversity. For example, Student A (see below) was a complete beginner when we started the project but the open, authentic nature of the task allowed him to demonstrate that he was starting to manipulate language to match circumstance:

Student work and translation: Job application texts

Student A (Words with errors underlined)

Job: (Blank)	In translating I have approximated the level of accuracy.
Ich heisse <u>Gotfleet</u> Raabe. Ich bin sechzig und in Australien geboren. Ich bin geboren <u>Oktober (funf)</u> 1901. <u>Der ist</u> vier Kinder , zwei S<u>o</u>hne und zwei T<u>o</u>chter. Sie sind zwanzig und junger. Ich bin stark und fleissig. Ich kann gut reparieren denn <u>I</u>ch bin mot<u>o</u>viert. Ich kann <u>arbeit</u> Montag,- Freitag vollzeitig, und teilzeitig Samstag und Sonntag. Ich bin ^ <u>gut</u> Mechaniker weil ich <u>bin erfahrung</u>, stark, mot<u>o</u>viert, freundlich und fleissig. *Danke,* *G. Raabe*	My name is Gottfried Raabe. I am sixty and born in Australia. I was born October (five) 1901. The is four children, two son and two daughter. They are twenty and younger. I am strong and hard-working. I am good at repairing and I am motivated. I can working full time Monday to Friday and part time on Saturdays and Sundays. I am good mechanic because I am experience, strong, motivated, friendly and hard working. *Thank you* *G. Raabe*

Students had never needed to write their German migrant names before so several misspelt them. In a few instances this student knew the vocabulary but mixed up the noun and verb forms or used singular forms instead of plurals; a few phrases sound more English than German, due to word order and over-condensing; but he would be understood. He does not rely solely on simple sentences and the work has an emerging sense of topic, relationship and mode in his persuasive tenor and his use of "Danke" and a signature.

Like most of those continuing their German from primary school, Student B, below, had initially demonstrated limited skill and confidence in using language (experiences appeared to be confined to traditional vocabulary sets such as weather, colours, numbers; mainly adjectives and nouns with little familiarity with colloquialisms, verbs or verb forms).

Student 4B

Job: Friseurin (Hairdresser)	
Ich bin funfzehn und in <u>meine</u> Familie Ich habe zwei Bruders und Schwester eine Vater und keine Mut<u>e</u>r. Mein Familie ist alter und <u>I</u>ch bin jung. Ich ^ gut <u>n</u>etzball ^ und Haare schneiden. Ich bin geboren in Australien funf Januar. Ich bin fleissig, hoflich, geschickt, erfahren und freundlich,_ <u>arbe</u> Ich bin kurz. Ich kann gut Haare schneiden und Ich <u>habe</u> gut Deutsch sprechen. Ich kann arbeiten vollzeitig Montag- Freitag, 8–17.00 Uhr. Ich kann beginnen sechs im Februar. Meine Famile ist vollzeitig und <u>I</u>ch bin motiviert. Ich kann arbeiten schnell.	1. I am 15 and in my family i have 2 brothers and sister a father and no mother. 2. My family is older and i am young. 3. I good at Netball and cutting hair. 4. I was born in Australia five January. 5. I am hard-working, polite, capable, experienced and friendly but I am short. 6. I can cut hair well and I have speak German well. 7. I can work full time Monday to Friday, 8–5. 8. I can begin six in February. 9. My family is full time (??) and I am motivated. 10. I can work fast.

The student has remembered many structures but is now attempting to manipulate them in different combinations and naturally makes errors. If we recognise that she always mis-capitalises Ich (I) and is very weak on dates, errors are relatively few. Several errors are obviously "in transit"; she often fails with a structure in one sentence but succeeds in another, as in her use of *haben* (to have) in sentences 1 and 6, of *kann* in 6, 7 and 8 and of *vollzeitig* (full time) in sentences 7 and 9, word order is sometimes, but not always, awry.

This task is designed to allow a student to write as much and as appropriately as s/he can and this student was inspired to call on all her second language resources to do this. She knows the meaning of a range of vocabulary and phrases which she uses to make richer meaning. This only misfires in sentence 9 which is incomprehensible. She has been creative with language in sentences 2, 5, 8 and especially 10.

Writing a letter is a traditional assessment task, and as students' comments above show, they are not all comfortable with writing tests. Nevertheless, the questionnaire which was done anonymously soon after this task indicated a continuing engagement in the language because of the drama and socio-cultural contextualisation.

> **T/R:** In the second term … Does anything stand out in your mind?
> **St 2:** I think it was the bits about the videos and that. I found them really interesting. I remembered about the Berlin Wall and all those kinds of videos and stuff.
> **T/R:** … Did you think that was a valid part of the learning to watch those videos?
> **St 2:** Yeah. That helped.
> **T/R:** Can you explain why you thought it was important?
> **St 2:** I guess it was interesting because it stuck in your head because it makes you think about like what would you be like … if you're like one of those immigrants, what would it be like? …

As the above job applications show, despite a widespread antipathy to written assessment, most of the students took it seriously and, as the final questionnaires demonstrate, it did not diminish their overall enthusiasm for the lessons. It was simply a part of a much wider experience facilitated by the drama work and its historical setting.

Conclusion

Intercultural language learning is part of learning new ways to live together in the world, experience which Neelands (2009) refers to as "being with", and such long term goals are not easy to relate to classroom assessment. However, in this project the assessment for learning model embedded in the process drama strategies promoted language learning in several ways.

Enrolment in the drama by students and teacher encouraged risk taking and participation so many students became more confident to experiment with limited language in order to communicate spontaneously. Actually "doing" drama allowed them to engage with both spoken and written language while also using their bodies as an expressive, communicative medium. Student commentary confirmed that this kinaesthetic element of the drama was a motivating factor for the assessment work. Student work, the video data and comments as exemplified above demonstrate how the dramatic enrolment led students to take all the tasks seriously, whether they were for formal grading or not.

Assessment modes included anecdotal records as in the hot seat; peer collaborative tasks as in the spontaneous part of the immigration interviews; and individual point in time assessment of all students as in the speech bubble, photo album, immigration interview and job application. From some student comments it seems that the opportunity for feedback by students through the research tools of interview and questionnaire also contributed to the nature of the assessment process, giving students a feeling of collaboration with each other and the teacher. As the video and written data demonstrate, the embedding of these assessment tasks in the dramatic learning sequence did enable all students to gain in confidence and to practise language in authentic situations. For many students it also developed their understanding of the power and complexity of language in intercultural situations.

References

Alexander, R. (ed. and lead author). (2010). *Children, their world, their education: Final report of the Cambridge Primary Review*. London: Routledge.

Black, P., & Wiliam, D. (1998). *Inside the black box: Raising standards through classroom assessment*. Retrieved 6.8.2010 from: www.questia.com/googleScholar.qst;jsessionid=MbjQkXkQQ0x5D9YTVyLvDYzL FQBnn9B3dnPfv8T0SSRGZ1fxVgV6!-1933696167!-2125728430?docId=5001380980

Byram, M. (1997). *Teaching and assessing intercultural competence*. Cleveland, OH: Multilingual Matters.

Neelands, J. (2009). Acting together: Ensemble as a democratic process in art and life. *Research in Drama Education, 14*(2), 173–189.

O'Toole, J. (1992). *The process of drama: Negotiating art and meaning*. London: Routledge.

Scarino, A., & Gould-Drakely, M. (2009). Assessing intercultural capability: Teacher and researcher perspectives. Paper presented at AFMLTA Conference 2009: *Dialogue Discourse Diversity*. Sydney.

Wyatt-Smith, C., & Cumming, J.J. (2009). *Educational assessment in the 21st century: Connecting theory and practice*. Dordrecht: Springer

Question A: Auf dem Schiiff: Photo album

Here are photos of the ship's voyage. If you wanted to make an album of the vo
photos would match which captions?

1.

2.

U.

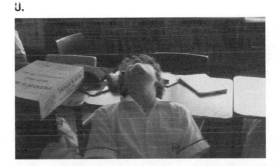

4

5.

6.

Write the number of the photo next to a caption (over page) which matches it.

Captions

a. Da sind nur zwei in dieser Familie. Das Kind ist sehr jung.
b. Da sind fünf in dieser Familie. Die drei Jungen sind glücklich.
c. Der Junge kann viele Vögel sehen.
d. Hier ist ein Familie von fünf Personen: ein Vater, zwei Jungen und zwei Schwestern.
e. Die Familie ist traurig. Sie sind alle deprimiert. Die Wellen sind groB, also ist ein Junge krank.
f. Hier sind eine Mutter und ihre Tochter. Die Mutter hielt ein Baby in den Armen.

Question B: Following ship's rules

a. You see this sign on the ship:

> # Auf dem Deck nicht schlafen: nur auf den Hängematten!

What would you do?

....

b. These signs are in the corridor:

| Männer | Frauen |

| Dusche |

Which one would you go into if you were seasick? Why?

....

c. Dieser Schild ist neben der Kabine des Kapitans.

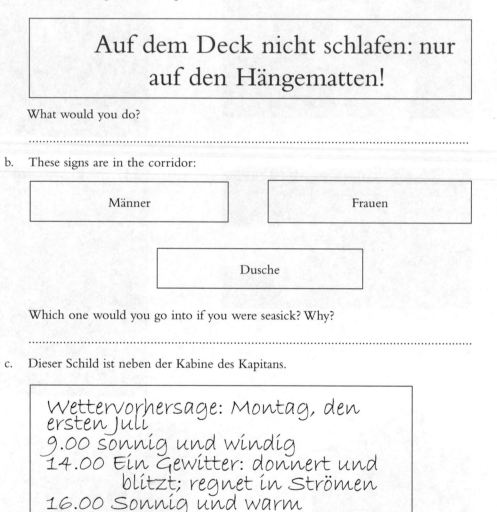

> Wettervorhersage: Montag, den ersten Juli
> 9.00 sonnig und windig
> 14.00 Ein Gewitter: donnert und blitzt; regnet in Strömen
> 16.00 Sonnig und warm

When would you go out and read on the deck?

....

6

Accessing Traditional Tales

The Legend of Bukit Merah

Madonna Stinson

This chapter focuses on the use of a familiar, traditional tale to engage students in language learning in a multilingual classroom context. The work described later in the chapter is an adaptation of a drama developed for Secondary Four students (up to sixteen years old) in Singapore. The drama was planned as the final set of three (of ten) lessons for a research study into the impact of process drama work on student results in the oral English examinations that every student in Singapore must undertake. I will describe and analyse the language learning opportunities afforded by the planned drama activities and interactions as students engaged with *The Legend of Bukit Merah.* At first I will explain the context for which the drama work was prepared and then go on to share the plan of the drama itself. Later I will discuss some influences and considerations that have been of importance to this work.

The context of this work

Singapore is an interesting place to work as a drama and language teacher. The language of schooling and business is English but the diversity of the population means that, for many of the inhabitants of Singapore, English is a second or third language. In this increasingly globalised world the governments of many countries in Asia have developed and implemented language education policies that focus on the connection between the capacity to communicate in English and the development of social and economic capital. Singapore, China, Hong Kong, Japan, Korea, Malaysia, Taiwan and Vietnam are among those nations with language education policies that make direct connections between the capacity to communicate in English and international relations and trade (Nunan, 2003). Additionally in Singapore, English is promoted as an interethnic language fostering ease of communication across Chinese, Malay, Indian and other ethnic groups who share no other common language.

A cornerstone of education policy is that English is the medium of instruction in school, from the preparatory years, through formal schooling to tertiary level, and the connections between effective use of English and economic and social capital are apparent in every facet of the society, from "Speak Good English" signs on the buses to political speeches. All this contributes to a particular social and political construction of language in the education system. Everyone in Singapore, it seems, rates the ability to communicate effectively in English very highly. The Ministry of Education English Language syllabus states that, by the end of their secondary education, students will be expected to be able to, "speak, write and make presentations in internationally acceptable English that is grammatical, fluent and appropriate for purpose, audience, context and culture" (Ministry of Education, 2001, p. 3), and progress is tested by national examinations in Primary Two (seven years), Primary Six (twelve years), and Secondary Four (sixteen years) levels. The results of these high-stakes tests in both written and oral English have a direct impact on students' educational and life paths, because they influence the placement of learners in ability-related "streams" of schooling at all levels of education. And all this is in the context of an educational system with students for whom English may be one of several languages and is often not spoken at home.

It was this educational context in which I found myself working in 2002. I am a monolingual (except for a smattering of French) Australian who worked in teacher education in Singapore from 2002 to 2009. During this time I began to think much more carefully about the issues of language and language acquisition in a bilingual and multilingual society like Singapore, and how these might affect my drama teaching practice. In my career as a drama and English teacher I have been conscious of the connection between the socially constructed nature of language, register, vocabulary, grammatical structures, and power and status. I have attempted to use a pedagogy which supports students to collaborate and learn from each other, to negotiate and contribute to their own learning, and find ways of making and expressing meaning about their own lives through drama. I realised that the language-focused drama work that I was doing was important and applicable to the culturally and linguistically diverse classrooms that we find in so many places throughout the world. As in Singapore, it is not uncommon in Australia and elsewhere, to be working with students who have English as a second or third language. For example, in my last Year Nine drama class in Brisbane, 2002, thirteen of the twenty-seven students were from first generation NESB (non-English-speaking-background) families.

The research

Research into drama and *second-language* learning (see, for example, Hoskisson & Tompkins, 1987; Kao & O'Neill, 1998; Wagner, 1998; Wilburn, 1992) has suggested that there is a range of benefits in the:

- contextualisation of language
- motivation, confidence and enthusiasm that drama promotes
- encouraging and safe atmosphere of the drama classroom
- shift in power from teachers to students.

My interest in researching this area grew out of reading Shin-Mei Kao and Cecily O'Neil's (1998) *Words into Worlds: Learning a Second Language through Process Drama*, which detailed a research project on Process Drama and language learning with beginning tertiary students in Taiwan. The text discusses a comprehensive and exciting approach that allows students opportunities to learn both *in* and *through* drama simultaneously and which moves beyond the tools and techniques approaches often employed as short-term activities in language classrooms. Rather than taking an instrumental approach to the teaching of language which relies on vocabulary and grammar-based games or role-based simulations of "real-life" activities, process drama offers a context and a purpose for language use.

I was able to pursue this interest by undertaking a research project that investigated the impact of process drama on oral communication with secondary school students. Ann Podlozny's (2000) meta-analysis had signalled that drama has a clear impact on oral communication skills, especially for older students, and I wanted to test that assertion out in my local context. For the research project in Singapore ten hours of drama lessons were planned, to be implemented by trained drama teachers in four schools in various locations across the island. The dramas were aimed at Secondary Four, "Normal Technical" (NT) students, a lower-ability stream, many of whom struggle to pass the written and oral public examinations in English.

The project included the detailed pre-planning of all drama lessons, training of facilitators and implementation of the ten lessons. Each lesson was taught by experienced, local drama teachers and designed to last for one hour. Data were collected via pre-tests and post-tests for randomly selected students from the intervention and comparison groups (the same students were tested on both occasions); facilitators' journals; and interviews with facilitators, the students' regular English teachers and additional randomly selected students. Our research question considered whether working in role within a Process Drama framework would develop the participants' oral communication skills. Students participated in four extended dramas, some of which required two or more hours, therefore some dramas lasted for two or three lessons.

Findings from the research

Statistical analyses of students' results showed a significant improvement in examination results in spoken English for students who participated in the drama classes, while the students in the comparison groups – those who were taught as usual in their English classes but had no drama experiences – showed no change (Stinson, 2008; Stinson & Freebody, 2006). In addition, all the drama students showed increased confidence in English-speaking contexts even outside their regular classes, and teachers noted that their students were much more collaborative and supportive of others within regular class contexts. One teacher who observed the drama classes said:

I could see how deeply the students were engaged in the activities and they were more talkative in my classes, too. They got on better with each other, and came up with their own ideas.

It is important to understand that none of the students who participated in the research had experience of drama as part of their regular English classes. Their teachers used quite formal, traditional strategies and approaches. When the drama classes began, the students seemed surprised and maybe even a little confused about this pedagogical approach. They participated dutifully and politely but didn't seem to commit greatly to the work. Perhaps they were developing trust in the process as a way of learning. However, following a few lessons (about six hours into the sequence) there was an intriguing shift in the dynamics of the classes, across the four school sites. From then on the students seemed to "get the hang of" the strategies and approaches, and became much more engaged, committed and productive in their work.

The Legend of Bukit Merah

The drama sequence that follows is an extended version of the plan that was used in the research project discussed here. The sequence should be considered as a suggestion only and can be adapted to suit your own classroom context. Although the drama was planned to work best when the sequence of activities is followed in order, the rate at which it is possible to move through the sequence may vary depending on the experience and interest of the students. The original sequence was divided into three one-hour blocks of time, so some activities that were used for re-focusing the students after a break or reflecting on the work done thus far, may not be essential if the whole sequence is completed within one block of time.

Resources needed

- A framed or mounted (at least A4) picture of the Sultan. This should be light enough to be easily carried about and propped against the wall or back of a chair. An alternative is to use a shadow puppet or a traditional marionette from the region if you have access to resources such as those.

- The story of *The Legend of Bukit Merah*. A complete version will be needed for teacher and students, as well as a version with the story divided into sections for small group work – see Episode 2.

- A large and ornate cushion or throne, or a chair that can be draped with some suitable fabric, e.g. batik.

The sequence

The sequence is offered in seven episodes, but that doesn't mean seven lessons. School and timetabling differences may mean that you will combine more than one episode into a lesson and some may require a break part way through. Try to make sure that each of your lesson sequences allows for some reflective time at the end. The time can be spent in whole or small group discussion, individual writing or drawing a reflective response to the lesson, or using a drama convention to highlight key moments, emotions or key learning. Reflection time allows us to identify what students have learned in the lesson they have just experienced and can be an important opportunity to model and develop a shared vocabulary as we talk about drama learning.

Episode 1
(Focus: speaking and listening, establishing the context, introducing power and status)

1. Students work in pairs. A can tell B to do whatever they want and B must do it. Reverse roles.
2. Students move about the space staying as far away from each other as possible. The teacher changes the tempo and quality of the movements but giving directions such as:
   - You are hurrying to meet your boss because you will be scolded if you are late.
   - Your boss has given you a task that you REALLY don't want to do.
   - You are heading home to the family after a long, hard day at work.
   - You are heading home to the family and your favourite dinner is ready.

   Finally:
   - You are the most powerful person in the world.

3. As the teacher counts backwards from ten the students gradually change to become the least powerful people in the world.
4. Place a chair in the centre of the room. It would be useful if the chair was ornate or could be made to look important, perhaps by draping it with fabric. Ask for a volunteer to sit in the chair as the most powerful person in the world.
5. The teacher reads aloud:
   Long ago lived a Sultan, the most rich and handsome in the land. No one could compare to him and, as time passed, he grew proud and haughty, always seeking praise. If others around him were praised for cleverness or acts of bravery he would become angry and vindictive. In fact, he would actually kill those who drew attention away from him.
6. One by one the students enter the space and say, "Your highness, if it please you, I will …" and offer something that aims to please the Sultan. If the offer pleases the "Sultan", they present/perform the offer, but if not, the "Sultan" clicks his fingers and the student "dies" in a dramatically violent and horrible way. If you have time, you might want to invite other students to take turns to sit in the Sultan's chair.

The lesson sequence starts with some warm-up activities that emphasize power and status. Feel free to substitute any others that you use regularly. Any one of these activities can be used or repeated as a focusing activity if you are breaking the sequence into blocks of time to suit your own school context e.g. 2 below can be used to introduce a broader range of characters in the story at the beginning of Episode 3, or to deepen commitment at the beginning of Episode 6. In each case the teacher would use characters (and events) from the story.

These activities offer opportunities for the students to use the language of "controlling" (Haseman & O'Toole, 1990) and related paralinguistic features as they follow instructions and make offers to the Sultan. They begin to use the vocabulary and language register of giving orders. In addition they are introduced to some of the roles in the story to be explored as well as the notion of limitless power. We will see the consequences of the latter as the drama unfolds.

A note: even though the language used in the story signals predominantly male characters, it is important to cast those roles "against type" to allow for implications of gender and personal attributes to be considered in the reflections at the end of each lesson.

Episode 2
(Focus: reading and listening, establishing the narrative, introducing tension)

1. Students are given a copy of the story and the teacher reads or retells the remainder of the text:

   One day, a school of fish with long, hard, razor sharp swords for noses swam to the shores of Singapura. They began leaping up and attacking the people on the beaches and the fishermen at sea. Their swords pierced right through the bodies of their victims. The Sultan took his army to the beach and saw the bodies of his people strewn across the once-white beaches now stained red with blood.

   He ordered his men to kneel and form a line on the beach, creating a wall against the swordfish, but the fish kept attacking. They continued to leap out of the water and kill the soldiers. After many of the men were killed, the Sultan called them to retreat and ordered that everyone stay away from the coastline.

   He gathered his advisors together and for days and days they tried to work out a way to deal with the problem, because Singapura was dependent on fishing and access to the sea for trade. After some time, a young boy asked for audience with the Sultan because he had an idea that he thought would solve the problem. He suggested, "Why don't we line the beaches with banana trees? When the swordfish attack, their swords will become stuck in the trunks and we can kill them."

   Everyone thought this was a wonderful idea and the people began cutting down banana trees. At the next low tide the Sultan's men planted them along the beach.

   The tide turned and the schools of swordfish approached. The Sultan, his men, the boy and many of the people of Singapura watched as the swordfish began attacking the line of banana stems, getting their snouts stuck in the thick stems. When the last swordfish became stuck, the Sultan's soldiers used their own sharp swords to kill every one of them. The problem was no longer.

You may wish the students to read the text silently and highlight, on the printed copy, key words or phrases that strike them in some way. I often then re-read the whole story and ask the students to join in when I come to the words they have highlighted. This "chorusing" supports both confident and developing readers.

The students should, by now, have a shared understanding of the story and be secure in the sequence of the narrative. The activities have required them to collaborate as they share ideas about how to prepare the freeze frames and how to encapsulate key ideas and issues in a single representation.

The people began to call out and praise the boy for his cleverness, saying that he was a blessing from the gods. The whole village celebrated with a fine meal of swordfish and much singing and dancing long into the night. As he heard the sounds of the celebration, the Sultan's heart filled with jealousy and rage.

The very next day he called the captain of his soldiers to him and ordered his soldiers to creep into the boy's home at night and kill him.

In the dark of the following night the soldiers went into the boy's home and began to stab him. As the boy began to scream in pain, his mattress filled with blood. The blood flowed over the sides of his bed and onto the ground. It kept on flowing and flowing. Even after the child was dead, the flow of blood did not stop, but spread down the hill, until finally it began to sink into the ground. The soil is still red today, and that is why the hill is called Bukit Merah (Red Hill).

2. Divide the class into small groups. Each group is given a section of the story and asked to create a freeze frame of that section. If you decide to share these with the whole class, tap in to selected students in each still image to hear them express thoughts and feelings at that instant in the story.

3. Each group decides on a caption for their freeze frame (and who will speak the caption) and the groups are arranged around the space in sequence. The story is then told in images and captions.

You may wish the students to read the text silently and highlight, on the printed copy, key words or phrases that strike them in some way. I often then re-read the whole story and ask the students to join in when I come to the words they have highlighted. This "chorusing" supports both confident and developing readers.

The students should, by now, have a shared understanding of the story and be secure in the sequence of the narrative. The activities have required them to collaborate as they share ideas about how to prepare the freeze frames and how to encapsulate key ideas and issues in a single representation.

Episode 3
(Focus: speaking and writing, considering roles and relationships)

1. Explain that you are going to explore some aspects of the story that we don't know much about and invite the students to agree to do this together.	At this point it is wise for the teacher to reinforce the collective agreement to pretend and remind the students that they are working within a fictional frame. Importantly, it commits the group to participate in the dramatic action that follows. Agreeing to pretend together provides a reason to speak and adhere to the language demands within the drama, and at the same time it diminishes the stress related to getting the language right because, "We are only pretending, after all."

2. Ask the students to list some "persons of significance" to the sultan. These people may not be named in the story but would be important to him in his life, e.g. the Captain of the Guard, the First Wife, a child of the sultan, a Chief Advisor, etc.	
3. In small groups create a role description for the characters, including – attitude to the event, power to persuade, and attitude toward the sultan. Add a phrase that the character might commonly use to the role description.	

Episode 4
(Focus: speaking and listening, deepening commitment and empathy within the drama)

1. As a large group draw a map of the location of the village. Mark in family homes and the location of the palace.	Drawing the map provides an opportunity to name specific places within the village and deepen the engagement of the students as they claim some of the space as their family home.
2. In small groups decide on roles within each family e.g. parent, grandparent, aunt/uncle. Make sure that each family grouping has one male child.	
3. Create a typical morning in the life of the village, with families breakfasting, greeting neighbours, cleaning, preparing for work etc.	The teacher can assist by musing aloud (in English) about what life would have been like in this time and location.
4. An announcement is made that the Sultan is on his way to inspect the village. Students, in family groups, must pay the proper homage to the Sultan as he moves around the space. The Chief Advisor [teacher-in-role] directs the homage to the Sultan. Emphasise the importance of pleasing the Sultan and also that the Advisor is sympathetic to the people in the village.	I use the picture of the Sultan here, rather than working in role. This allows me to take on the role of the Chief Advisor, which is important later. The teacher-in-role as the advisor is able to model vocabulary and language register as they escort the Sultan through the village. There is an aspect of ritual in this episode, which enhances the power of the sultan and raises the stakes for the families in the village.
5. Take a break from role and discuss responses to what is going on in the drama so far.	

Episode 5	
(Focus: speaking and listening, increasing the tension, adding a complication)	
1. Back in the village, the villagers are going about their daily business, discussing the Sultan and how indebted they are to the boy. Freeze. 2. Teacher narration: *One of the servants from the palace rushed to the village with terrible news: the Sultan had heard the villagers speaking so well of the boy. He was furious because he saw this as a betrayal. He had decided to kill all the young boys in the village as a way of punishing them for their disloyalty.* 3. Out of role the students discuss strategies that the villagers might use to save their sons' lives. 4. Everyone back in role. The Chief Advisoer (teacher-in-role) offers to help them try to reason with the Sultan. He offers to set up meetings with significant people who have influence with him. 5. Students choose three or four of the people (from the list drawn up earlier) who might be able to influence the Sultan. They form new groups – one for each of the chosen roles – and rehearse the arguments that might be put to them. The teacher can move about the groups and challenge student ideas through questioning.	The tension has increased in this episode, as the students recognise what is at stake for each of the families. The group's knowledge of the Sultan's decision complicates their relationships with each other and with the Sultan. The requirement for commitment is heightened. Students with varying language capabilities are supported by having an opportunity to plan and rehearse arguments that hope to persuade the Sultan to change his mind. This allows all students to contribute confidently as they consciously consider and select vocabulary, and refine sentence structures in order to impress and influence the sultan. They negotiate with the advisor and consider the nexus between relationships, status and influence.

Episode 6	
(Focus: speaking and listening, considering alternative viewpoints)	
1. Change of roles. It is the eve of the night that the Captain has been ordered to kill the boy. No one knows whether the Sultan has been persuaded to change his mind or not. Students, in the groups that have prepared the arguments for the Sultan, take up the collective role of that individual in a designated space in the room. Each of them is thinking of the arguments that they presented to the Sultan, and repeats an action that the character might perform, e.g. the Captain sits and sharpens his sword, the First Wife combs her long hair, the Sultan's son tosses a small ball repeatedly in the air, the Chief Advisor writes down the events of the day, or other suggestions from the students.	In this activity the teacher operates as a volume control. As the teacher moves closer to one of the students-in-role it is as though the volume has been turned up, the student speaks aloud a word or phrase that indicates his/her thoughts or feelings, and, as the teacher moves away the volume is turned down. Thus we hear the arguments that are meant to persuade the sultan to change his mind about the killing of the boy. For example the Captain[s] might say: *It is not sharp enough yet. I need this to be quick; I am an honourable solder and will follow orders; My son is the same age; or he might simply say Tonight, when it is dark …*

2. Ask the students to lie down for a few moments of sleep.	In these activities the students draw on the information they have contributed to the drama up to this point as they suggest the thoughts and feelings of influential characters. In practice, even though they know the ending of the story, there is always a gasp when the narration conforms to the original narrative.
3. Teacher narration: *It was the quietest of nights. No breeze stirred the palm leaves. The night birds were silent and the frogs had ceased croaking. It seemed as if the whole world was holding its breath, hoping that dawn would not come. In the dark of this night the sultan's men went to the boy's home and began to stab him. His mattress filled with blood which kept on flowing and flowing. Even after the child was dead, the flow of blood did not stop, but spread down the hill, until finally it began to sink into the ground. The soil is still red today, and that is why we call the hill, Bukit Merah (Red Hill).*	
4. Derole and debrief.	The deroling and debriefing is important in this episode because it allows for emotional distancing from the event. To derole you may say something like: *Out of role as I count back from 10.* Debriefing involves talking about what happened in the drama and how participants felt.

Episode 7 (Focus: speaking and listening, reading and writing, reflecting on the narrative)	
1. The local museum wants to commemorate the legend of Bukit Merah by creating an interactive display that tells the story, using multiple voices. As a large group discuss the characters and events that the students believe are important to include in the museum display. List these and add details about how each section of the display might be presented.	This episode allows for discussion about how the students would LIKE the legend to be represented. Often it differs from the rather romantic perception of the story that they are familiar with.
2. In small groups, students prepare a segment for the interactive display. The segments may take many forms e.g. rehearsed performances of events from the story; "talking heads" as individual characters share phrases or monologues; projections of digitally recorded images; soundscapes/wordscapes; or documentary-style narrations.	Talking heads: Individual students or small groups present short monologues or dialogues which share their part of the story.

Soundscapes/wordscapes: almost like the soundtrack of a movie but may include words or phrases. |
| 3. Set up the exhibition. | You may wish to use this as an opportunity to invite another class to see what the students have produced. |

Why use traditional tales?

In this case the students who were part of the research study came from assorted cultural and linguistic backgrounds but had the story of Bukit Merah in common. The story provided a shared platform on which experiences and understandings were built as the series of lessons progressed. When the story sequence and the roles and relationships are familiar, students are more easily supported "to ask and answer questions, to solve problems, to offer both information and opinions, to argue and persuade" (Kao & O'Neill, 1998, p. 25). The platform of the shared story encourages students to be more confident as they experiment with vocabulary and speech patterns. They find safety in the familiar narrative structure because they know what is coming next and they are working with known roles and relationships and vocabulary held in common. Drama strategies make it possible to step off the platform of the familiar and move into situations which require spontaneous interactions and language use. It is the latter which allows us to access our personal, mental dictionaries and, as one student said, "I found I could use words I didn't even know I knew."

Planning for drama and language learning

Here I would like to offer some considerations for planning language learning opportunities within a drama frame:

> Depending on the language capabilities of the students, a you may either insist that only English will be spoken during the lesson, or allow students to work in common language groups at times to plan.

> It is beneficial for each lesson to include opportunities for students to work in and out of role, in small and large groups, and participate in activities where collaboration is essential to solve problems within the developing drama.

> Change the constructions of groups regularly so that participants are constantly working with, and will need to communicate with, new group members. This ensures they are not always collaborating with their usual friendship (and language) group and provides opportunities to interact with classmates with whom they would not regularly interact.

> Plan lessons so that every student has at least one significant opportunity to speak in each. In this way they become accustomed to speaking in front of others and develop confidence in using new vocabulary and correct pronunciation.

> Include experiences where students are required to react and respond to questions or situations without any prior preparation so that they became used to engaging in spontaneous speech acts.

> Use a range of different language registers and purposes within the dramas.

> Include reflection time at the end of each lesson where the students can talk about how they feel about the work and what they have learned.

There are a number of challenges for language teachers wishing to use extended drama work: drama can be time-consuming and complex in both preparation and implementation. The most effective drama is slow enough for deep inquiry and intriguing enough to sustain interest over time, even when that time is broken into discrete lesson periods. When students are more used to formal and traditional language teaching strategies, we need to allow sufficient time to develop familiarity and confidence with the processes and forms of the learning medium.

Drama is based in play and, while learning in drama can be serious and seriously hard work, it also draws on our capacity for playfulness in the creation of the fictional worlds that our role-playing inhabits. Play is not commonly part of the pedagogy in many international classrooms, and some students may resist drama activities because they do not understand that learning is taking place. Therefore the reflection phase of each lesson is vital. This allows for teacher and students to identify the language learning that has taken place and helps to recognise that play and learning are not mutually exclusive.

A final point that must be made is that teachers benefit from professional development that develops their understanding of and skill in implementing the drama process. Few ESL teachers are trained for this way of working.

By working in role and in the fictional "as if" context of drama, students have opportunities to create new contexts, to create fictional roles and viewpoints, to develop relationships, to respond to the language demands of the dramatic situation while in role, and to practise "real-life" language in the safe space of dramatic fiction. "Drama provides a reason to use language", says Miccoli (2003, p. 22). Language learning opportunities are enhanced when drama provides a framework for learning and a context for communication. The dramatic frame motivates students because they have something to say and a reason for saying it. In the fictional world of the drama, students can rehearse language in a way that mirrors the unpredictability of the real world with its "coughs and hesitations" (Holden, 1981, p. 2). It allows for many right answers and opportunities to rehearse those answers. By entering into the fictional world students are able to draw parallels and make connections to their own world.

References

Haseman, B., & O'Toole, J. (1990). *Communicate Live!: Exploring the functions of spoken language.* Melbourne: Heinemann Educational Australia.

Holden, S. (1981). *Drama in English language teaching.* London: Longman.

Hoskisson, K., & Tompkins, G. (1987). *Language Arts: Content and teaching strategies.* Columbus, OH: Merrill.

Kao, S.-M., & O'Neill, C. (1998). *Words into Worlds: Learning a second language through process drama.* Stanford, CT: Ablex Publishing.

Miccoli, L. (2003). English through drama for oral skills development. *English Language Teachers Journal, 57*(2), 122.

Ministry of Education. (2001). *English Language Syllabus 2001 for Primary and Secondary Schools.* Singapore: MOE.

Nunan, D. (2003). The impact of English as a global language: Policies and practices in the Asia-Pacific Region. *TESOL Quarterly, 37,* 589–613.

Podlozny, A. (2000). Strengthening verbal skills through the use of classroom drama: A clear link. *The Journal of Aesthetic Education, 34*(3–4), 239–275.

Stinson, M. (2008). Drama, Process Drama and TESOL. In M. Anderson, J. Hughes, & J. Manuel (Eds), *Drama in English Teaching: Imagination, action and engagement* (pp. 192–212). Melbourne: Oxford University Press.

Stinson, M., & Freebody, K. (2006). The DOL project: An investigation into the contribution of process drama to improved results in English oral communication. *Youth Theatre Journal, 20,* 27–41.

Wagner, B. J. (1998). *Educational drama and language arts: What research shows.* Portsmouth, NH: Heinemann.

Wilburn, D. (1992). Learning through drama in the immersion classroom. In E. B. Bernhardt (Ed.), *Life in language immersion classrooms* (pp. 67–83). Bristol: Multilingual Matters.

7

Insights From a Drama-EAL Classroom

Using Drama with English Language Learners in a Canadian High School

Burcu Yaman Ntelioglou

Reflecting on my own experiences as a non-native speaker of English and French, and as a teacher of ESL and EFL, I recognize the possibilities that lie in combining imagination, language, culture and identity, making the use of drama an especially important component of second language classrooms. When I first used drama in my language classrooms many years ago, I was surprised by how much scope it provided for my students to express themselves. I couldn't exactly point to why drama was so effective, but I knew that it was helping my students to take more risks, to participate in classroom discussions, to share their ideas and experiences more openly and to use language in new ways. Recently, as an educator and researcher focusing on drama teaching and learning with English language learners – especially in highly multicultural and multilingual contexts – I had the opportunity to observe a carefully designed Drama-EAL course in a highly multicultural Canadian high school for one year as part of a larger research project.

This chapter focuses on the use of drama with language learners in this Drama-EAL course. The class is offered for students for whom English is an additional language. Its students come from diverse cultural and linguistic backgrounds (e.g., Afghanistan, Albania, Bangladesh, China, Colombia, Ethiopia, Haiti, Iran, Iraq, Korea, Mexico, Russia, Sri Lanka and Taiwan). The course runs for two hours every day for a period of nine weeks, which they label as one "quad". The goal in this class is to use drama strategies to improve students' English language skills. All students in this classroom have some proficiency in English and enter this publicly funded high school after passing a proficiency exam. For most of them drama is very new, therefore they are slowly introduced to drama activities that reinforce both verbal and non-verbal communication in English. In this chapter I will describe the content of this course and outline the strategies it makes use of.

Physical and vocal warm-up activities

Three major drama units are presented in this course. In order, they are: a tableau unit, a scripted role-play unit and a storytelling unit. It is important to mention that one of the first things the students experience in the very first week of their Drama-EAL class is physicality (getting up on their feet and doing warm-up activities such as Atom 3[1] or building the tallest tower, in groups, using straws). They also do vocal warm-ups to get comfortable using their voices. These warm-up games, such as asking the students to line up according to the day and month of their birth day starting from the beginning of January to the end of December; or lining up according to the alphabetical sequence (A to Z) of their names; or People Bingo,[2] are methods the teacher uses to try to interest the students in getting to know each other and in recognizing their individual personal and cultural backgrounds.

Physical and vocal warm-up activities continue throughout the nine weeks. Interviews with the students revealed that these warm-up activities are not only important to help them get used to moving about and feeling more comfortable in the drama activities to follow, but also very important to help them wake up, since the class starts at 8:30 in the morning. The teacher in this class is especially skilled in making use of these activities to teach English, as well as to make students feel comfortable with their bodies. For example, she combines vocabulary learning and pronunciation with warm-up activities. Earlier in the course, before introducing a warm-up activity where she needs to use the names of various body parts, she distributes to the students a list of anatomical terms. She goes over that list, paying attention to the meaning of each word as well as its pronunciation. Then students, in groups, make a human-size body image using flipchart papers and note different parts of the body on this image. This helps them learn the necessary vocabulary to understand instructions for different physical warm-up activities.

Students recognize that vocal warm-up activities assist them with their pronunciation, stress and intonation. They find these vocal warm-up activities especially rewarding when the teacher focuses on the sounds, syllables, words or phrases that are most challenging for the different language speakers in that specific classroom. I found that during these vocal warm-ups even the shyest students who are reluctant to speak show willingness to take a risk and yell out the words, phrases or syllables that the teacher would like them to repeat.

Tableau unit

The task in this unit is for students to work in small groups to create a series of tableaux (frozen images) to tell a story based on a folktale. For this unit, students as a class first discuss different elements of a story such as setting, characters, plot and climax. They then learn about what a tableau is and discuss elements important in a tableau. Then each group is asked to choose a different story from *World Folktales: An anthology of multicultural folk literature* (Stern, 1994). A concept like this is especially valuable in this class, with students from many different cultures, because it validates students' different backgrounds. Students read the story they choose a couple of times, both individually and as a group, and then answer some comprehension questions. They then fill in a "Story Outline" handout that asks them about the setting (when and where), characters, initiating problem, sequence of events and solution of the story. What is particularly effective about this concretizing exercise is that students brainstorm together not only in order to understand the story well but also to start thinking about the scenes in the story that are most apt for them to portray as tableaux. Students are also invited to use costumes, props or set pieces if they like. Students work on this task for a couple of days. Then they present the tableaux they have created to the class.

I find that students taking this course treat these tasks very seriously and produce good quality work. Some of their seriousness and respect for the task may result from the fact that they are graded for this presentation. But I think a more likely reason for students to value what they are doing and work on it seriously is the teacher herself, who models engagement by being very enthusiastic, serious and explicit about what she is teaching and why. The teacher always outlines tasks very clearly and distributes handouts describing what the students need to accomplish. For example, she informs students very early about the marking criteria and this is very beneficial for them as they now know exactly what they need to prepare. This teacher informs them that for this presentation she is going to give them a group mark (out of 10), an individual mark (out of 10) and a participation mark (out of 10). She specifies that for the group mark she is going to pay attention to the clarity of plot; elements of tableau (such as levels and blocking); precision of tableau; set up and transitions. For the individual mark she will pay attention to characterization as well as facial and body expressions. The participation mark enables her to grade not only the end product but also the process. She informs the students that for the participation mark she will pay attention to group dynamics and group use of preparation time as well as how individual students work within the group and the extent to which they make a positive contribution to the work.

Students then are given a chance to reflect on their presentation and group work process as they write a two-page journal response to each unit. Many drama researchers have written about the value of writing journal responses as a post-presentation activity. Pioneering drama practitioner Dorothy Heathcote once stated that experience alone without reflection will not lead to learning. Through my observations, however, I have seen that it is not always easy for students to write successful personal responses unless they are guided in this process. Students have a tendency to write a summary or a list of what their group did first, second, third and so on, instead of presenting an analysis of what they have done personally; what their group has done; how they felt; what worked; and what didn't work. Therefore in order to guide these students without restraining them, their teacher gives them a list of questions they can reflect on such as: "What did you find the most difficult part in creating tableaux and why?" "In doing tableaux what do you think your strongest skill is?" "Is there anything you would change about your performance during the presentation or preparation process?" Journal writing helps these students to think critically and fosters meta-thinking, since through reflective writing students take the opportunity to analyse their embodied experience, assumptions, values and their learning throughout this process. On interviewing students, I found that what makes this reflective writing process even more engaging for them is the prompt written feedback to their journal reflections that they receive from their teacher. She hands back the journals with elaborated responses within a week and students appreciate this written dialogue that takes place between them and their teacher. Through this dialogue, the teacher, too, learns more about the students and their meta-thinking and has a chance to respond to the strengths of their personal reflections as well as to any questions or difficulties the students might be experiencing during the unit.

Scripted role play unit

Before moving to the major task in this unit, the teacher introduces the difference between improvised role-play and scripted role-play through two different smaller tasks. For the first task students try out improvised role-playing in pairs. The teacher hands out a small piece of card to each pair. On the card there is a situation. For example: "An employee wants to use his/her vacation days on a certain week and the boss is not willing to give those days off." Another card says: "You and your friend are supposed to be doing a research paper together. You have done a lot of work, but your friend has done nothing. Tell your friend how you feel." The pairs decide on a scene and present it to the class. For the second task, in order to introduce scripted role-play, the teacher uses a very short (two-page) script called *Fly Soup*, written for English language learners. At the end of the script there are a couple of comprehension questions. The script is appropriate to the English proficiency level of these students and does not have any difficult vocabulary or grammatical structures. There are six characters in the script and each character speaks short lines. The script provides students with a context to use both verbal and non-verbal language. I present below a short excerpt from the beginning of the script.

FLY SOUP
Characters: Henry Smith
A waiter
Customer 1
Customer 2
The restaurant manager
Scene: A crowded New York restaurant
Henry: Waiter. Waiter!

(*The waiter comes up to Henry*)

Waiter: Yes?
Henry: There's a fly in my soup!
Waiter: That's impossible.
Henry: Look.
Waiter: Where?
Henry: There. What's that? (*He points to a speck in the soup.*)
Waiter: What? (*He leans over to look at the soup.*)
Henry: That little black speck with wings. What's that? (*He points to a fly.*)
Waiter: Black pepper! It's black pepper!
Henry: It is NOT black pepper. It's a fly!

(*The customers crowd around the table.*)

Customer 1:   What's wrong?
Customer 2:   What's the matter?

The script ends when Henry accidentally drops a box of flies from his pocket. The manager realizes the trick and kicks Henry out of his restaurant.

Before the students are asked to practise the script as a group, they first read it individually, then a couple of volunteers read it out loud to the class. After going over the comprehension questions and leading a brief discussion about the script, the teacher divides the class into groups of six to practise it. Because of the humour in the script there are lots of giggles as the students prepare to perform. The next day all groups present their role-play to the class. Students are not graded for these two exercises. Yet the teacher provides constructive feedback after each presentation and helps them to think carefully about characters, situation, setting, mood, the conflict, resolution and props so that they become aware of all of these elements as they get ready for their major task in this unit. I find that it is extremely important for teachers to model giving constructive feedback so that when students are invited to give feedback on each other's work, they know how to offer respectful and productive comments. When this process of giving feedback is done right in a drama classroom, the discussions after the presentations become rich and very valuable for student learning. This positive classroom atmosphere also helps to maintain a safe zone for students to both give and receive feedback.

After these two smaller performance tasks, the teacher prepares students for the main task in this unit. That day the class begins with a discussion about holidays and celebrations such as Mother's day, religious holidays, Victoria Day (a Canadian statutory holiday celebrated in honour of both Queen Victoria's birthday and the current reigning Canadian sovereign's official birthday), Valentine's Day and so on. The teacher brings a handout with newspaper articles about different festivals around the world such as Christmas, Chanukah (the eight-day Jewish holiday), Eid-al Fitr (Muslim festival) and Kwanzaa (a seven-day festival held in the USA that begins on 26 December, celebrating African heritage). She also gives them a handout with a cross word puzzle made of holiday celebration vocabulary.

Students read the information on the handouts, do the puzzle and then are invited to share their favourite celebrations in their country of origin or in Canada. They discuss differences and similarities among different celebrations and, because their teacher shows the utmost care in ensuring that everybody is respectful in their comments, students are quite willing to share information. For this task students are put into groups of five or six. Together they write a short play about a celebration of their choice. The celebration can be Canadian or one from a different culture. The teacher reminds them that there must be conflict in the story and resolution, and hands out guidelines to help them outline the script. These ask them to write three scenes: the first being the invitation scene, the second the preparation scene and the third the celebration scene. The guidelines also tell them first of all to brainstorm ideas as a group; to improvise these ideas; then to write the play together. They are asked to give a copy of their play to the teacher so that she can edit it and photocopy the script for each member of the group. The students are then given plenty of time to rehearse their three scenes before presenting their performances to the class during the presentation day. Each group presents their performance to the class and receives feedback from the teacher and their classmates. Students also receive grades for their performances. As with the tableau unit, the teacher again informs students early on about the marking criteria and she gives them a group mark (out of 10), an individual mark (out of 10) and a participation mark (out of 10).

Here I would like to share an excerpt from the script that one of the groups wrote. The students in this group first shared what their favourite celebration was and why. Then they decided that they were going to write about the Eid celebration. Two of them were familiar with Eid and they explained that it is important to help neighbours in need during Eid. One of them shared a personal story about this; the other members of the group found the story very appealing so they decided to perform it.

A REAL EID
Characters:
Mr Ahmed (Father)
Mrs Ahmed (Mother)
Sana (Daughter, 18 years old)
Sidra (Daughter, 15 years old)
Asif (Son, 12 years old)
Umar (Poor Boy / Asif's friend, 13 years old)

Scene 1
(Moon sighting night: Mr and Mrs Ahmed are sitting on the sofa and watching TV. Sidra is fixing cartons and Asif is helping her. Sana is doing some work in the kitchen.)

Asif: Hey guys! Aren't you going to see the Eid crescent moon?
Sana: I am going to the roof. Who wants to come with me?

(Sidra and Asif shout together)

Sidra & Asif :   We are coming too.

(Mrs Ahmed stops doing her work in the kitchen and says to Mr Ahmed)

Mrs Ahmed: Let's go to see the moon with the children

(They both head towards the roof.)

Asif: I see it! I see it!
Sidra: Where?
Asif: There. *(pointing to the moon)* Don't you see? It is above the tree.
Sidra: I see it now. It is there *(Sidra pointing to the moon.)*
Sana: I can't find it.
Sidra: It is just on the right of the tallest building.
Sana: Yes! Yes! I see it too.

(Everybody greeting each other saying "Chaand Mubarak")

Mrs Ahmed: Guys, let's do everything fast. Tomorrow will be Eid and we don't have much time to prepare.
Sana: We have almost finished everything. Now Sidra and I are going to put henna on our hands.
Asif: Sister, can I do henna on my hands too?
Sana: No Asif , only girls can apply henna on their hands

(Everybody is moving downstairs. Suddenly Mr Ahmed sees a child outside the house and he seems very sad)

Mr Ahmed: Who is this boy?

(Mrs Ahmed and Asif stop to see the boy)

Mrs Ahmed: He is our neighbour.
Mr Ahmed: Why is he looking so sad?
Mrs Ahmed: I don't have any idea. Let's talk to him.

The script then continues with Mrs and Mr Ahmed learning from the boy that he is sad because he doesn't have new clothes, shoes or other new things for Eid since his family can't afford it. Since all the shops are already closed because of the Eid celebrations, the son decides to give this boy the new clothes and gifts that he received himself for Eid, and they also decide to give money to this family. The boy and his parents get really happy when they receive the gifts. The script ends by everybody celebrating the Eid party at this family's home.

As seen in this short excerpt from one group's script, students learned the elements of script such as the list of all characters, the description of the setting, stage directions, dialogue and also learned to divide their script into three different scenes. Students also made use of the language used in the example script (*Fly Soup*) that their teacher provided them with earlier. For example, the dialogue from the student script includes some lines directly from *Fly Soup,* such as: "I see it, I see it!" "Where?" "There!"

Storytelling unit

As I mentioned earlier, doing drama, speaking in front of the public, and performing are all new experiences to most of these students. Therefore this course is designed gradually to increase their confidence in standing and speaking in front of others. With the tableau unit, they first get used to standing up and being comfortable with their body language. The tableau unit does not require them to communicate verbally and this is a huge relief to most of these students, since they are just getting used to this course. Students tell me that the role-play unit helps them with their verbal communication. They start to build confidence speaking in front of others, improving their pronunciation, and controlling their voices since most of them speak very softly the first few times they practise their role-play. Students think that performing as a group of five or six helps during the performance because, even if somebody forgets a line, that person can improvise and present the information in another way.

In order for students to get comfortable telling a story, before introducing the main task in this unit, the teacher asks each student to bring an object that is special for them and to explain why, in a couple of sentences. After this short exercise, which is not graded but is meant to prepare the students for their storytelling performance, the teacher introduces the main storytelling task. Usually the main storytelling task is the most difficult one for these students because for this they work in pairs. They return to Stern's (1994) book of folktales from around the world, but must choose a different story than the one they used for their tableaux. Each pair tells a story to the class with one partner telling the first half, and the other telling the second half. While doing this, the pairs face the audience and do not use any notes. The teacher models how telling a story is very different from reading a story aloud, because storytelling requires more personal interaction between the storyteller and the audience. The goal in this task is for them not to *act* a story but to *tell* it using their own words, illustrating different characters and emotions in the story through the use of their voice alone. Students are encouraged to use props or costumes if they wish, and are informed that clear content, concentration, clear pronunciation, eye contact with the audience and a good level of volume are key elements that the teacher will be looking for during the storytelling.

To help students break down the story and decide what parts are important to tell, to organize their story and to help them to learn it, the teacher provides a handout. It includes space to write a short introduction and a conclusion, and there is also a series of boxes where they can jot down the main events they will need to remember. In order to make the story their own, students are encouraged to change words or add voices, sounds or gestures to make it come alive. The teacher underlines the importance of practice, encouraging them to rehearse it several times in order to feel comfortable in front of the class. Finally, as was the case in the first two units, students are asked to write a journal entry expressing how they felt before, during and after their storytelling presentation. During post-interviews several weeks after the course, students told me that it was nerve-racking to try to tell a story in English to an audience for the first time, but now that they know the tools to present a story all by themselves, they felt far more confident about the presentations they will have to do in front of a class in future high school or post-secondary courses.

Integration of different language skills through drama

Drama tasks in this course certainly provide a meaningful basis for developing students' language skills. Different language skills are integrated throughout the units. For example for the tableau unit, students first have to read a story, answer comprehension questions and learn vocabulary that they find difficult. They work on this first individually. Then as a group they discuss their answers and any questions they might have regarding the story, and write summaries, deciding what parts of the story they are going to focus on in the series of tableaux they will create. Therefore this task allows them to practise the language skills of reading comprehension, vocabulary, summary writing and interactive listening and speaking. For the role-play unit they write more intensively and focus more on their speaking as they memorize and perform their own lines in front of the class. Here they are called upon to pay attention to both their verbal communication and non-verbal/ paralinguistic skills, such as their physical movements, gestures and facial expressions. For the storytelling unit, they have to select and read a story carefully, make sure they understand the vocabulary and write it in their own words. They are called upon to focus on good pronunciation as well as the tone and volume of their voice. The journal writing that they do after each unit helps them to think critically and use deeper levels of analysis in their writing. In all of these units the teacher explicitly informs the students which skills the various drama activities are helping them practise.

Challenges, conclusions and implications for teaching and learning

Each group of students I observed in every nine-week session had slightly different interests and needs, and the teacher was flexible to make sure that these were met. Of course, there were often challenges that needed to be addressed, and key among these was the issue of grouping. Most of the drama tasks involved group work and the teacher's approach was sometimes to let students form their own groups and at other times to form the groups herself. A few students complained, however, because certain students were often absent and this was affecting the quality of their work. Others complained that one or two students were dominating discussions and were not willing to negotiate their ideas. The teacher responded by encouraging students to write brief reflections about their group work process. Their reflective writing would inform her about group dynamics, but more importantly make students more aware of their individual contributions to group work. She also prepared guiding questions to help them, such as: "What do you feel are your strengths when working with your group?" "What makes you a good participant in your group?" "You have worked together for one day. Do you think that your group will work well together? Why or why not?" "In one sentence describe the character you'll perform in the role-play." "What is the mood or tone your group wants to create with the tableaux?" "Did your group rehearse well?" "Do you feel your group is prepared for your presentation? Why or why not?" "Do you feel confident about your role(s) in the role-play? Why or why not?" "What can you do to help yourself feel more confident?" The teacher found that students were quite honest about their group participation and the group dynamics. She also thought that this reflective writing process helped certain students to do better in the future tasks in this drama class. These reflections informed the teacher so that she could help students or groups that might need extra support. In their journals students stated that even the challenges that they faced during group work taught them valuable lessons and tools for the future. Below is an excerpt from Nelly's journal expressing some of the struggles she faced working as part of a group and what she made of that challenging experience:

> *Well I was very surprised for the team performance. I was thinking that this presentation was going to be a disaster, yes DISASTER! But to my surprise it was very satisfactory.*
>
> *When I saw my name in the paper with other names in my group, I told myself ☹ "OK Nelly this looks hard to do … it looks like big challenge" (and it was). During four long days we were talking and talking and changing and changing everything because one of the team members was doing something while the other member was doing something else … We were not acting like a team. Finally we were able to practice the presentation from start to end once and it was good. I mean really good. But the day of the presentation again the same two team members forgot their things for the performance (surprise!), yes the costumes and other special things for the presentation. Yes, the day of the presentation! I was very disappointed but, fortunately the rest of the members saved the presentation. I was very very happy and proud of the team for the beautiful performance of each one. After that I was thinking to myself "Nelly, every situation has a challenge and Thank God because he teaches me that every day."*
>
> (Nelly's role-play unit journal entry, April 2009)

Nelly also chose to reflect on this challenge, referring to it as her most memorable experience. In this final reflection she writes that this challenging experience helped her to be more open minded in working with different people from different backgrounds.

> *My most memorable experience in this classroom was the role-play performance about the "celebrations". It was a very big challenge that I described in my Journal #3. In this presentation I had many feelings but in the end I learned a lot from this experience. I learned about working with different people with different backgrounds and gained from everybody and every situation in the classroom and made new friends. It made me open more my mind. And in the end I can say that it was a very very good experience. ☺*
>
> (Nelly's final journal entry – End of class reflection, April 2009)

What stayed with me the most after my year-long observations in this Drama-EAL classroom was the palpable energy and active engagement that was present throughout the course. When drama is used effectively in a language class – as was the case here – students immerse themselves in the tasks and become more willing to communicate, take risks and try new ways of expressing themselves in the language they are learning. In all of these three units, students were given choices and opportunities to become included in the tasks. Through the use of creativity, imagination and interpretation, they prepared and performed works that they themselves came up with. They were genuinely engaged, personally invested and took their tasks seriously.

For language learners to take drama tasks seriously and to resist immediate stereotypical improvisations in student work, it is important for the teacher both to model quality work and to mention explicitly the specific drama and language skills the students will be developing as they work on their drama tasks. What is also extremely valuable is providing students with written guidelines or graphic organizers to help them think deeply and critically about what they are working on. During post-course interviews, many students spoke of how much they appreciated how drama had provided a space for them to learn about others and themselves through cooperative work, collaboration and the sharing of personal reflections. It was a space especially valuable for these groups of English language learners, since both the country and the language were new to them. Students stressed that if it was not for the friendly and welcoming space that the drama course provided for them, then they would not have developed the same confidence and courage they now had in their ability to learn English. Theatre has long been known to build a sense of camaraderie among its participants. However it is important to understand that even a drama class can become a space for animosity if the teacher is not careful to make sure that students respect and value each other's comments and contributions, and to ensure that they negotiate ideas as they work on tasks that require team work.

Although the needs, goals and content of every course and every group of language learners in a class are different, it is my hope that the insights provided in this chapter will be useful for teachers interested in using drama to help the development of language skills. I would like to end this chapter with a few quotations from students expressing their appreciation for the supportive community fostered in this drama course, as these quotations are representative of the feelings of many of their classmates.

> *Because of group work I feel much better about my English because I made many friends and explored how other students think and speak when we work in group team.*
> (Student journal entry, March 2009)

> *I am very happy I worked with different persons from different cultures and gained from every person. I made new friends and I opened more my mind. This was very good for me and for my English.*
> (Student journal entry, June 2009)

> *I love conversations and group work in drama. I made new friends from different countries and each of them taught me new things.*
> (Student journal entry, June 2009)

> *Drama class was an unforgettable experience for me. I never thought I can talk with others in English. I made lot of new friends and I liked working with team. They helped me. I helped them. Working in small groups and doing drama and presenting together is best way to improve English. At the beginning when I spoke in group, they didn't understand. Day by day my English was getting better. They help my English. I help them. Now I know that I can speak, even tell a story in English well and not be shy.*
> (Student interview, May, 2009)

Acknowledgements

I would like to acknowledge and thank the teacher and the students in this Drama–EAL class for their willingness to share their thoughts, feelings and lived experiences with me.

Notes

1   Atom 3 is a warm-up activity that helps students to mingle. Students first walk around the space randomly. They must not bump into one another as they walk. The teacher then calls out "Atom [and then a number]". Students have to form groups of this number with others nearest to them. Students must group into this number as fast as possible. A good trick is to call "Atom 1". The teacher can also use this warm-up activity to form groups for the next activity. When the teacher calls out a number for the last time, she/he can call out the number she/he wants the groups to be in for the next activity.

2   People Bingo: The teacher hands out a sheet to each student with a list of questions such as: What are your hobbies?; What is your first language?; How many languages do you speak?; Which countries have you visited?; Which cities have you seen?; How long have you been living in Canada?; Can you play a musical instrument?; Do you like to cook? If yes, what kind of food do you like to cook?; Do you have a pet? What kind of pet is and what is its name? and so on. Students ask one of these questions to any student in the class. They then write the name of that classmate and the answer their classmate gives. The goal is to meet and ask a question of as many classmates as possible. Since this specific classroom is very large, with about 50 students each quad, this activity gives the students a chance to get to know their classmates.

Reference

Stern, A. (1994). *World folktales: An anthology of multicultural folk literature.* Lincolnwood, IL: National Textbook Company.

8

Using Drama to Enrich School-Based Assessment in the Hong Kong Secondary School English Language Classroom

Tanya Kempston

The problem with a lot of English teaching in Hong Kong is that it is really boring. That is not to say that teachers are boring. But when you have 40 students in front of you in a crowded classroom and you have to do something with them, and next lesson there will be another set of 40 students and another 40 after that, well, the easiest thing to do is to cover a few more pages in the textbook and finish the syllabus. And set compositions and mark them. Now, the problem with this new SBA is that we teachers are supposed to encourage students to read and enjoy reading. With all the other things we have to do, now this as well?

(Comments made by a teacher participant in the
*Thinking and Acting Creatively in the English
Classroom* workshop held at the University
of Hong Kong in January 2010)

Introduction

In 2006, 95% of the Hong Kong Special Administrative Region (HKSAR) population was ethnically Chinese (Hong Kong SAR Government, 2006, p. 5). Also, '93.9% of Chinese aged 5 and over usually spoke Cantonese at home, followed by other Chinese dialects (other than Cantonese and Putonghua) (4.6%), Putonghua (0.9%) and English (0.5%).' (p. 36). It is evident that Cantonese is the first language of many Hong Kongers. However, under the HKSAR government's 'bi-lingual and tri-literate' policy, English is one of the languages Hong Kong young people are supposed to acquire and enhance in the course of their primary and secondary education (Hong Kong Education Bureau website 2010).

Education in Hong Kong has undergone significant reform since the year 2000. The 'Learning for Life, Learning through Life' consultative document noted that 'learning is still examination-driven … school life is monotonous, students are not given comprehensive learning experiences with little room to think, explore and create' (Education Commission 2000, p. 6). It is perhaps not surprising that learning is examination-driven (and, in my experience as a worker in the secondary sector in Hong Kong, textbook-driven) given the transmission model of learning in which the 'teacher and textbook are seen as authoritative sources of knowledge … learning will take place through dedication and hard work, through close attention to texts and memorization' (Jin & Cortazzi 1998 p. 102). They further note that this learning model 'has a long cultural history in China' (p. 102).

Following the publication of the Education Commission document, and since September 2009, secondary schooling in Hong Kong[1] has been organised into two parts: Junior and Senior, both of which will consist of a three year course of study. Students will now take the Hong Kong Diploma of Secondary Education (HKDSE) at the end of senior secondary school instead of Advanced Level (AL) examinations. However, the aim of the reform is not simply to effect structural change but to revitalise education in Hong Kong and to 'enable every person to … develop in the domains of ethics, intellect, physique, social skills and aesthetics, so that he/she is capable of innovating and adapting to change; filled with self-confidence and team spirit' (Jin & Cortazzi, p. 6).

The place of drama in secondary school education in Hong Kong

Drama 'has long existed as a successful extra-curricular activity in schools' in Hong Kong (Hong Kong Arts Centre 2004, p. 11). Plays staged to celebrate school anniversaries or as part of a school's annual tradition, dramatic duologues performed during the annual Hong Kong Speech Festival, productions acted out during the course of the annual Hong Kong Schools Drama Festival … drama with a polished final outcome or product continues to thrive in the Hong Kong secondary school community.[2] However, with the implementation of the New Senior Secondary (NSS) mode of education, drama is now present in the formal curriculum. Although it is not available as a discrete subject, secondary schools can offer an elective called 'Learning English through Drama' as part of the English subject all students must take and be assessed on. While it is encouraging that drama has got a foot through the door of the Hong Kong curriculum, this elective is something of a missed opportunity in terms of curricular innovation. It foregrounds the learning of theatrical terminology, scriptwriting and performance of student-scripted role plays rather than recognising or including opportunities for drama as a pedagogical method. Knowledge about, legitimation of and the use of drama as an organic process in the traditions espoused by practitioners such as Heathcote (1976), Bolton (1979), O'Toole (1992), O'Neill (1995), Wagner (1999) and Neelands (2010) is still emergent in Hong Kong schools.

Process drama is increasingly being recognised and documented as a potentially powerful pedagogy for second language teaching and learning (Kao and O'Neill 1998; Liu 2002; Stinson & Freebody 2005). During my involvement in teacher education in Hong Kong, I have repeatedly seen many students and teachers realise that, when engaging in workshops using process drama conventions, this type of activity is not only joyful but purposeful and productive. They have also articulated doubt as to whether such playful activities could achieve accepted 'mainstream status' as methods for learning in Hong Kong schools given the (still) exam-orientated nature of the Hong Kong education system. However, the changing nature of the Hong Kong education system has created possibilities for the 'giant at the door' (O'Toole, Stinson & Moore 2009) to slip through a window of opportunity into the comfortable room of mainstream curricular legitimacy. One of these windows is the School–Based Assessment element in the English subject.

School-Based Assessment

As part of the new Senior Secondary English curriculum, all secondary students must undergo School–Based Assessment or SBA in a number of subjects, including English Language. According to the Hong Kong Examinations and Assessment Authority (HKEAA) as part of SBA in English:

- Students will read/view a number of texts (including books, films and documentaries) over the course of study and;

- They will take part in group discussions and make individual presentations based on what they have read/viewed.

(HKEAA 2008)

These group discussions and individual presentations on the texts, which comprise a total of 10% of the total percentage of 15% allocated to SBA within the English subject, take place over three years during which students study for the Hong Kong Diploma of Secondary Education. Teachers are responsible for assessing SBA in their schools.

One of the difficulties with SBA, as another workshop participant pointed out, is that students are all too aware that the group interaction and presentation will be assessed and that this assessment comprises part of the final grade for English. Thus, as the same participant noted, 'students know they have to read or watch and understand the texts, but lose any sense of enjoyment of or interaction with the text … reading is just a means to an end, the text is just another thing to get out of the way.'

Process drama within School-Based Assessment activities

On the basis that drama is a well-documented way in which individuals can inhabit a text and mine its layers of meaning beyond simple semantic decoding, a workshop for in-service teachers was devised. It had the following aims:

- Participants would explore and begin a process of imaginative inhabitation of a text of similar linguistic difficulty to one recommended for School–Based Assessment through process drama conventions.

- Participants would discuss how and the extent to which such process drama techniques could be used in their own teaching context.

After the reassurance that no-one would be forced to be an 'actor' and following several warm-up activities, the teachers played the part of concerned villagers, small business owners and members of a primary school's Board of Governors. How uninhibited individuals can become, both in their actions and language when in role in the 'no-penalty zone' described by Heathcote (1976, p. 171) was evident in the workshop. This workshop, according to one teacher, 'was unexpected as it involved no scripts but there was plenty of writing, talking and listening and real communication, which is what we hope our students will get better at!'

In the discussion following the process drama scenario in which participants looked at ways in which some of the techniques could be implemented in their schools, some participants remarked that they did not expect to enjoy themselves as much as they had done. Others said that such an enjoyable process might be regarded with distrust back at their school, as laughter could be taken as a 'sign of playing and not working' by school authorities. In the rest of this chapter, I have attempted to address some of the concerns of the teacher participants who were open to the idea of trying process drama strategies in language learning, but who were also cognisant of the difficulties of successfully conducting these strategies. Participant questions in the post-workshop discussions and their relation to implications for classroom practice are also examined.

The format of the process drama scenario

The context for the scenario which followed the initial warm-up games was based on 'The Great Mouse Plot' chapter from Roald Dahl's autobiography *Boy* (1986). This chapter was chosen as it offers plenty of opportunities for rich dramatic response and, in terms of language use and linguistic difficulty, is similar to another Dahl text approved by the Hong Kong Examinations and Assessment Authority.[3]

Warming-up

I enjoyed the warm-up games, but how could I carry these out with my own students? Would there be chaos? Would the teachers in the room next to me complain?

(Teacher Participant)

Participation in warm-up activities has been well documented as a necessary pre-requisite for successful drama (Kempe and Nicholson 2007; Neelands 2010; Winston & Tandy 1998). After taking part in several energetic games and quieter, less strenuous warm-up activities adapted from Winston and Tandy (1998), the participants seemed more relaxed and ready for the imaginative scenario to follow. They had clearly enjoyed the warm-ups. However, a common concern for the participants was that such activities could quickly spiral into chaos in a real-life school situation. The participants were all used to teaching classes of forty or more students in what they agreed were relatively small rooms. It was agreed that some of the physical games could be dangerous in this type of environment. The participants were quick to come up with their own solutions. For instance, if students could be divided into a split class of approximately twenty students, then more was physically possible in the regular classroom. It was also suggested that quieter, small-scale mime activities were also appropriate in such a classroom. Also, a whole class (of forty or more students) could be taken to the school Activity Room[4] for drama activities.

Into the process

A 'lively pre-text' (O'Neill 1995) is essential for drama to succeed as a pedagogical method. Workshop participants were shown PowerPoint pictures of the village of Llandaff and were then led to a village 'sweetshop' in another corner of the room in which a sign saying 'Closed', a (rubber) mouse and various sweets, including gobstoppers, spilled out of a large glass jar and lay on the floor alongside a few pencils and scraps of paper. They were asked to assume the role of concerned villagers and small business owners and to discuss what they thought had happened at the scene and write down these speculations. The teachers noted that these artefacts immediately set the scene for what was going to follow and a 'scene of the crime' context such as this would be possible to arrange even in a regular classroom, although it would be better if students could move around the scene even more freely.

Following a short period of discussion and speculation about what had happened, I assumed the role of a stern school Principal. Participants were told that the sweetshop owner, Mrs Pratchett, had just visited my primary school and accused some of the Primary Five boys of planting a mouse in a sweet jar. The teachers stayed in role and were invited to a meeting at the local school with 'Mrs Pratchett' (I would assume this role later) to find out more about her claim that the boys had planted a mouse on her premises.

Following the meeting with Mrs Pratchett (teacher-in-role), during which I took on the role of a mean-spirited elderly lady who particularly disliked primary school students, one participant was invited to take on the role of 'Dahl'. Dahl, one of the accused mouse-planters, was hot-seated by the other workshop participants in role as 'concerned members of the school Board of Governors'. Dahl was subsequently questioned about his role in the affair. During the hot-seating, Dahl admitted his guilt but also let slip that his friends had been present when the mouse had been planted in the sweet jar. After this confession, the 'villagers' (participants-in-role) again met the 'Principal' (workshop leader-in-role) and decided what, if any, punishment would be meted out to the boys involved in the Great Mouse Plot. Participants were then asked to write a brief description of these punishments in an adaptation of a role-on-the-wall exercise (Neelands and Goode 2000, p. 22). They examined these descriptions and ranked the punishments from least to most severe.

I then appeared in role as Dahl and after looking at the range of punishments on the wall, pleaded for leniency for myself and my friends, saying that Mrs Pratchett's rudeness and lack of hygiene had led me to concoct the Great Mouse Plot. Finally, the participants were asked to assume the role of Dahl and write a letter of apology to the cantankerous sweetshop owner. After this final written task, the teachers engaged in a reflection exercise to finish off the process. During this group sculpture exercise (ibid., p. 79), participants formed three groups of five and one 'sculptor' modelled the group members into a tableau containing Dahl and one of his schoolmates, the school Principal and two villagers after the letter of apology had been handed over. One group modelled their tableau while other groups observed and thought of a word to encapsulate the scene.

After the scenario had concluded, the participants read 'The Great Mouse Plot' chapter on which the scenario had been based and compared the events in the chapter with the process drama sequence. They also shared the three written tasks they had completed in the scenario. Finally, they discussed how the different strategies used in the drama could be implemented in their individual school contexts.

Implications for classroom practice

Can process drama also be used in regular classroom teaching as well as SBA?
(Workshop Participant)

In the post-workshop discussion, the participants agreed that such a situation provided students with a valuable opportunity to voice their own responses to the text in a playful environment, deepen their understanding and respond to the text in a creative manner.

There was consensus that process drama techniques could be useful in he
inhabit the world of the text more fully through interaction with each o
would have to engage with the text beyond simply reading it and preparing
one teacher called 'a glorified book report presentation, which is not likel
exciting for them or their classmates' for their Assessment.

The teachers mentioned that their students had a wide range of proficiency in English
from near-beginner to very good. It was agreed that when interacting in their second language, students would need more wait-time and think-time before responding in imaginative
scenarios. However, the need for allowing plenty of wait and think-time was, as one teacher
said, necessary if he were asking his students questions in a regular English classroom situation.
The teacher-in role as Principal strategy was mentioned as being not difficult to carry out,
as 'We teachers are also sometimes authority figures' – a comment from one participant.
Teachers noted that their students would enjoy and be motivated to use English in the scenario they had experienced themselves. Teachers also noted that although they might be
willing to try out these techniques with students, the support of school authorities if using
drama to help students engage with texts chosen for School-Based Assessment was essential.

'I wish there could be more playful activities like this. We have a textbook to cover as
well as School-Based Assessment and we have to cover the items of English students will
need to know in the public exam.' This comment reflected the pressure teachers experience as deliverers of textbook-based content and all the participants noted that the textbook was the basis for most lessons they taught. 'Not using the textbook is not an option'
as one person noted. I would like to elaborate on this issue rather than simply suggest that
process drama only has relevance in a limited School-Based Assessment 'play corner'.

Textbooks can be useful tools in second language acquisition and can help learners
acquire the target language in predictable sequences. Over-reliance on textbooks can also
kill any interest in language learning. In her discussion of literature as an aid in second lan
guage learning, Spack (1985) quotes Widdowson's comment, 'Textbooks are full of fiction.
Mr and Mrs Brown, son David, daughter Mary pursuing the dreary round of their diurnal
life' (1982, p. 205). English teaching and learning is, from the accounts of in-service teachers
taking part in the workshop, pressured and often dull for teachers and students alike.
Exposure to authentic texts via School-Based Assessment may help to overcome some of
the apathy to English engendered by the sole use of textbooks in language learning.

It was my experience teaching in a government-subsidised Hong Kong secondary
school that there was great pressure for teachers and students to 'cover the textbook'
especially in the period before tests and examinations. Language teaching and learning,
from the anecdotes of teachers I heard when I moved into teacher education, very often
seemed to be strongly influenced by Behaviourist approaches developed from Skinner
(1957). This approach, among other things, emphasises accuracy, repetition in the form
of drills and the avoidance of errors. For students and teachers (including me), this meant
a process of rigid adherence to textbook centred on practices such as the hasty explana-
tion and drilling of students in totally uncontextualised grammatical and lexical items.
Stepping outside this accepted paradigm of teaching and learning meant that the teacher
ran the risk of censure from school authorities. In addition to this, opportunities for
speaking outside the rehearsal of scripted textbook dialogues were rare.

Although textbooks are carefully designed, learning English only through them would
indeed be a bland linguistic diet! Hence, the introduction of School-Based Assessment
and the opportunities to use interesting, *authentic* texts is an innovation to be welcomed.
Simply 'covering the textbook' perpetuates the 'jiao shu', or 'teach the textbook' (Jin and

Cortazzi 1998, p. 102) cycle of teaching and, I would contend, has negative consequences for students' English language development, especially in respect to mastery of the productive skills. If students only have the opportunity to learn English from textbooks, they may memorise target forms quickly but have little, if any, opportunity to experience other forms of richly varied input from their co-learners.

Stephen Krashen's proposed 'monitor model' (1982) has relevance here. In his 'input hypothesis', L2 acquisition occurs through exposure to *comprehensible input*. If such input contains structure and forms just beyond the learners' current level of competence in the language (this is called i + 1 by Krashen), then both understanding and acquisition will occur. In the workshop situation, for example, the teachers reacted in role to the idea that the sweetshop might have been broken into, as this exchange shows:

Michael (Bakery owner):	Well, look at this, you can see candy everywhere …
Gail (Clothes shop owner):	Perhaps it was some, ah, you know, thieves.
Michael:	Breaking into the sweetshop, but why is this rat here, why would the hooligans kill a rat?
Gail:	Hooligans, what do you mean? I don't know … that word.
Michael:	I mean, people causing destruction because they can.
Gail:	Oh … yeah. Maybe.

Here, Gail seemed to be exposed to and acquire a new word, 'hooligans', when in role and engaged in conversation with Michael. Second language learners may, in Krashen's Acquisition-Learning hypothesis, '*learn* via a conscious process of study and attention to form and rule learning' but *acquire* language as we are exposed to samples of the second language which we understand' (Lightbown and Spada 1999, p. 38). From the example above, drama scenarios which allow students to interact with texts in an organic fashion also allow for the acquisition of unknown language items through the medium of unscripted spoken discourse.

As the workshop participants experienced, the drama was unique in that no other group of individuals would have responded in exactly the same way in the scenario. The teachers had to communicate and collaborate in unscripted, genuine responses to the stimulus to help move the drama along. Therefore, the willingness to use textbooks as genuine pre-texts and springboards for communication rather than simply asking students to memorise the content of the course book is essential. In response to the evolving secondary school curriculum, textbooks used in Hong Kong EFL classrooms are changing. Many textbooks now include richly authentic texts such as poems and short stories in addition to the characters engaged in their fictitious 'diurnal round'. If teachers can and are allowed to make use of such texts in innovative ways, including as pre-texts for process drama, then spoken discourse of a genuine nature between students can occur.

Integration of specific language items within process drama

Students would enjoy many of these activities in School-Based Assessment preparation. However, the fact remains that there are many grammar items which need to be taught in preparation for examinations. How can I integrate them with process drama activities?

This comment was voiced by one teacher. However, all participants responded to it, either by nodding, saying 'Yes' or looking at me for my response. Front-line teachers such as those who attended the workshop know that students' acquisition of and ability to use grammatical and lexical items will be tested in school and public examinations.

In their book *Drama Techniques* (2005), Maley and Duff outline many useful drama activities to consolidate language learners' understanding of discrete grammatical items. However, process drama is very often carried out according to a narrative sequence. I would suggest that teachers look carefully at a sequence to see how it can be divided into coherent episodes. Each episode, like an act of a play or a television serial, could use process drama strategies to progress the unfolding of the narrative sequence and, importantly, would end at an exciting moment with multiple possibilities for the drama to carry on in the next and future episodes.

Grammatical and lexical items could then be introduced, practised and consolidated within these episodes. Although debates on the value of inductional versus deductional approaches to grammar instruction (Shaffer 1989) still continue, Terrell's (1991) conceptualisation of a three-step Explicit Grammar Instruction method or EGI would be useful in helping structure the acquisition of language items within such an episode. Terrell states that:

> EGI can affect the acquisition process in three different ways:
>
> 1) as an 'advance organizer' to aid in comprehending and segmenting the input;
> 2) as a meaning-form focuser that aids the learner in establishing a meaning-form relationship for morphologically complex forms; and
> 3) by providing forms for monitoring, which, in turn, will be available for acquisition in the output.
>
> (Terrell 1991, p. 58)

This EGI model has correspondences with the objectives of the 'Learning Grammar in Context' section of the *English Language Curriculum and Assessment Guide for Secondary 4–6*. In the *Guide*:

> Task-based learning does not preclude the learning and teaching of grammar. Fluency and accuracy are complementary … grammar is seen as a means to an end and it is not taught as a system of rules or a stand-alone body of knowledge. For the learning of grammar to be effective, learners must be given ample opportunities to apply their knowledge of grammar in interaction and communication.
>
> (Curriculum Development Council and HKEAA 2007, p. 75)

With the overarching principles of interaction and communication in meaningful situations informing the nature of what students will be asked to do, Episode One could, therefore, be organised as follows:

Pre-text set-up

Students view PowerPoint pictures of the village of Llandaff and are then led to a village 'sweetshop' in another corner of the room. They view the artefacts scattered on the floor: a sign saying 'Closed', a (rubber) rat and sweets spilling out of a large glass jar on the floor alongside a few pencils and scraps of paper. This pre-text set-up is the part of general 'advance organiser' which provides the overall organising structure for the grammatical and lexical input.

Students-in-role

This is when steps 2 and 3 in Terrell's model can be carried out. Students assume the role of concerned villagers and small business owners and discuss what they think has happened at the scene. However, before writing down these speculations, they are introduced to the modal verb 'could' and its function as a way to show possibility (meaning-form focusing). The teacher can model the use of the form and provide examples related to the sweetshop situation (providing forms for monitoring). Students then write down their speculations: the teacher can move from being a drama facilitator to language facilitator and make appropriate suggestions and corrections. To practise the use of 'could' and to move the action on, students can then verbally share their speculations with the other 'villagers' – the target forms mentioned by Terrell are available for acquisition or output in this sharing.

Teacher-in-role

Following the sharing of these speculations, the teacher assumes the role of school Principal and tells the participants that the sweetshop owner, Mrs Pratchett, has just visited our primary school and accused some of the Primary Five boys of planting a rat in a sweet jar. Participants stay in role as villagers and are invited to a meeting at the local school with 'Mrs Pratchett' (the teacher can assume this role later) to find out more about her claim that the boys had planted a rat on her premises. This will set the scene for a second episode in which the teacher-facilitator gets into role as Mrs Pratchett and one of the boys involved in 'The Great Mouse Plot' is hot-seated.

Advantages of the process drama episode

The advantage of drama's plasticity is that it can be stretched and stitched in such a way so as to allow explicit instruction to be enfolded into the playful fabric of the imaginative context. The strong contextualisation of the grammar item to be learnt and used in Episode One does slow down the flow of the dramatic action to some extent but, crucially, gives students the opportunity to practise the modal both in written and oral form. However, teaching and learning about the modal 'could' need not take up the entire duration of the Episode. It is up to the discretion of the teacher how long the EGI component should take.

Opportunities for writing and grammar learning

A wide variety of grammatical and lexical items could potentially be introduced and practised in this episodic structure. Within 'The Great Mouse Plot' process drama scenario, there are at least four opportunities for grammar learning and writing using the EGI model. The first, in Episode One, has been discussed. In the second, students could describe an appropriate punishment for the students involved in the 'Mouse Plot' and can practise forms such as the modal 'should' to express obligation or verb phrases when describing punishments. For example, 'You should be made to clean the classroom floor every day for a week!' The third task could require a description of a possible punishment for Dahl, the instigator of the Great Mouse Plot. This is a useful opportunity to practise appropriate collocations, for instance, 'It is *crystal clear* that you have been naughty and must be punished.'

The fourth, a letter of apology from Dahl to the sweetshop owner Mrs Pratchett, affords opportunities for practising verb–subject agreement. For example, if practising the rule that a singular verb should be used with periods of time or sums of money, students could first correct the statement, 'Two years cleaning the windows of your sweetshop are a high price to pay' (ought to be *is*). They can then, in role as Dahl, devise their own responses to the punishments that were devised in the third task. The *English Language Curriculum and Assessment Guide (Secondary 4–6)* notes, 'Learners should be helped to see the connection between forms and functions and internalize the forms through meaningful…use' (Curriculum Development Council and HKEAA 2007, p. 75). These activities draw upon students' creation of and involvement in the scenario and allow for the integration of target grammar and lexical items in their own responses to the scenario.

It is reasonable to assume that students will make mistakes when acquiring and using the target language. Doing so is a normal aspect of language learning. However, as teachers commented after the workshop, making mistakes in front of one's peers is not necessarily an enjoyable part of the process. As the teachers experienced during the workshop, mistakes can be made but the affective power of the drama allows one to perform in the L2 with dignity and confidence. Here Krashen's affective filter hypothesis (1982) is particularly relevant in respect to the effect drama can have as a language learning strategy. According to Krashen, the imaginary barrier of the affective filter prevents learners from acquiring language from the available input. A learner who is bored, anxious or tense may put up a linguistic filter, thus blocking input. Drama can significantly lower the affective filter. As one teacher commented, 'English is my second language and I make mistakes, but today I didn't mind making them so much because I was enjoying myself. I think my students would enjoy this and learn something too.'

Final thoughts

The potential of drama as a medium for richly meaningful language learning in the Hong Kong EFL context has not yet been fully realised. It has an important role to play in helping students engage with texts set for School-Based Assessment as well textbooks. That students would communicate with each other in an authentic way – trying ideas, making mistakes and responding to suggestions – during a process drama scenario was evident to the professionals who participated in the workshop.

'In order to know oneself, one has to communicate' (*zhiji zhibi, huxiang goutong*). This Chinese saying is a potent reminder that the act of communication, whether in one's first or second language, is an integral part of knowing oneself and responding to the wider world. As a relatively new pedagogy in language learning in Hong Kong, process drama techniques need to be tried, shared and adapted by teachers. It has an important part to play not just in the teaching and learning of English as a foreign language but in developing students' understanding of themselves, the texts with which they engage and the world in which they must interact. It would indeed be a shame if drama were to remain in a neatly sealed, extra-curricular context and not used to the fullest extent.

Acknowledgements

My thanks to all those who participated in the *Thinking and Acting Creatively in the English Classroom* workshop held at the University of Hong Kong in January 2010, who let me include excerpts from the workshop as well as their comments in this chapter.

Notes

1　R.M.H. Cheng notes the existence of 'government, aided, direct subsidy and English Schools Foundation and private schools' in Hong Kong and says that the majority of schools are publicly funded but privately run' (Cheng 2004, p. 535).
2　The community referred to here is the one composed of government-aided and directly subsidised schools referred to by Cheng (2004). These schools will offer the HKDSE. English Schools Foundation or ESF schools as well as other international schools offer drama as a separate subject.
3　Dahl's *The Witches* is on the list of the *Recommended Texts for SBA* (2009) document issued by the Hong Kong Examinations Authority.
4　Most secondary schools in Hong Kong have a large indoor multi-purpose space besides other communal spaces such as the covered playground or Assembly Hall. Such multi-purpose spaces are usually big enough to allow at least one 'normal' class of forty or more students to move around freely.

References

Bolton, G. (1979). *Towards a theory of drama in education*. London: Longman.

Cheng, R.M.H. (2004). Moral education in Hong Kong: Confucian-parental, Christian-religious and liberal-civic influences. *Journal of Moral Education, 33*(4), 533–551.

Curriculum Development Council & Hong Kong Examinations and Assessment Authority (2007). *English Language Curriculum Guide (Secondary 4–6)*. Hong Kong: Hong Kong SAR government printer.

Dahl, R. (1986). *Boy: Tales of childhood*. London: Puffin.

Education Commission. (2000). *Learning for life, learning through life: Reform proposals for the education system in Hong Kong*. Hong Kong: Education Department.

Heathcote, D. (1976). Drama as a process for change. In L. Johnson, & C. O'Neill (Eds.), *Dorothy Heathcote: Collected writings on education and drama* (1984) (pp. 114–126). Cheltenham: Stanley Thornes.

Hong Kong Arts Centre. (2004). *Developing drama-in-education report*. Hong Kong: The Art School, Hong Kong Arts Centre.

Hong Kong Education Bureau. (2010). *Policy highlights – primary and secondary education*. Available at: www.edb.gov.hk/index.aspx?nodeID=139&langno=1. Last accessed 18/04/2011.

Hong Kong Examinations and Assessment Authority (HKEAA). (2008). *Hong Kong Diploma of Secondary Education Examination: Information on School-Based Assessment*. Available at: www.hkeaa.edu.hk/DocLibrary/Media/Leaflets/SBA_pamphlet_E_web.pdf. Last accessed: 18/04/2011.

Hong Kong Examinations and Assessment Authority (2009) *HKDSE English Language: Recommended texts for the School-Based Assessment component*. Available at: www.hkeaa.edu.hk/DocLibrary/SBA/HKDSE/Eng-SBA_Recommended_Texts-091008.pdf. Last accessed: 18/04/2011.

Hong Kong SAR Government, Census and Statistics Department. (2006). *Hong Kong 2006 Population by-census thematic report: Ethnic minorities*. Available online at: www.bycensus2006.gov.hk/en/data/data2/index.htm. Last accessed: 18/04/2011.

Jin, Lixian, & Cortazzi, M. (1998). The culture a learner brings: a bridge or a barrier? In M. Byram, & M. Fleming (Eds.), *Language learning in intercultural perspective: Approaches through drama and ethnography* (pp. 98–118). Cambridge: Cambridge University Press.

Kao, S.M., & O'Neill, C. (1998). *Words into worlds: Learning a second language through process drama*. Stanford, CT: Ablex Publishing.

Kempe, A., & Nicholson, H. (2007). *Learning to teach drama 11–18* (2nd ed.). London: Continuum.

Krashen, S. (1982). *Principles and practice in second language acquisition*. New York: Prentice Hall.

Lightbown, P.M., & Spada, N. (1999). *How languages are learned*. Oxford: Oxford University Press.

Liu, Jun. (2002). Process drama in second- and foreign-language classrooms. In Gerd Bräuer (Ed.), *Body and Language: Intercultural learning through drama* (pp. 51–70). Westport, CT: Ablex Publishing.

Maley, M., & Duff, M. (2005). *Drama techniques* (3rd ed.). Cambridge: Cambridge University Press.

Neelands, J. (2010) *Beginning Drama 11–14* (3rd ed.). London: Routledge.

Neelands, J., & Goode, T. (2000). *Structuring drama work* (2nd ed.). Cambridge: Cambridge University Press.

O'Neill, C. (1995). *Drama worlds: A framework for process drama*. Portsmouth, NH: Heinemann.

O'Toole, J. (1992). *The process of drama: Negotiating art and meaning*. London: Routledge.

O'Toole, J., Stinson, M., & Moore, T. (2009). *Drama and curriculum: A giant at the door*. Dortrecht: Springer.

Shaffer, C. (1989). A comparison of inductive and deductive approaches to teaching foreign languages. *The Modern Language Journal, 73*(4), 395–403.

Skinner, B.F. (1957). *Verbal behaviour*. New York: Appleton-Century Crofts.

Terrell, T.D. (1991). The role of grammar instruction in a communicative approach. *The Modern Language Journal, 75*(1), 52–63.

Wagner, B.J. (1999). *Building moral communities through educational drama*. Stanford, CT: Ablex Publishing.

Widdowson, H.G. (1982). The use of literature. In M. Hines, & W. Rutherford (Eds.) *On TESOL'81* (pp. 203–214). Washington, DC: TESOL cited in: Spack, R. (1985). Literature, reading, writing and ESL: Bridging the gaps. *TESOL Quarterly, 19*(4), 703–725.

Winston, J., & Tandy, M. (1998). *Beginning drama 4–11*. London: David Fulton.

9

Second Language Learning and Cultural Empowerment

Teaching Shakespeare in Taiwan

Astrid Yi-Mei Cheng and Joe Winston

The unit of work described in this chapter was taught to a class of seventeen year-old female students learning English at an advanced level in a senior high school in Taiwan. It was part of a doctoral research project investigating how drama pedagogy can engage and promote various aspects of language learning and how these dramatic approaches resonate with current theories of teaching and learning second languages. In Taiwan, textbooks at this level mostly consist of expository writings organized around factual information. Although there is nothing wrong with expository texts per se, their prevalence does not sufficiently enhance the linguistic competence and cognitive skills of able students. We believe that literary texts rich in poetry, metaphor and cultural references can serve not only to enrich their language but also to further their enthusiasm for learning the language.

In Taiwan, the senior high school system serves as a preparatory stage for higher education. For these students, access to this kind of learning resource is particularly significant as they are entitled to know and have access to the culture of power. Learning Shakespeare, international literary and cultural icon that he is, can therefore serve both political and linguistic purposes. It is not uncommon, of course, to hear that Shakespearean language is daunting and a cause for anxiety even for students in English speaking countries. However, our contention is that this need not necessarily be the case for able students learning English as a 'foreign' language; and that the challenge of learning complex, literary texts might, indeed, enhance the pleasure they experience in learning it.

The social and interactive nature of drama resonates with a sociocultural view of language, a view that has been growing in significance in the field of Second Language Acquisition over recent years (Firth & Wagner 1997; Freeman & Cameron, 2008; Lantolf 2000). Sociolinguistics holds that language is learned *through* interaction rather than experienced in isolation; and that it functions in relation to 'scenarios' or in 'contexts of situation'.

Influenced greatly by the work of Halliday (1978) they hold that three dimensions determine the semiotic structure of a situation type and that these three dimensions – field, tenor, and mode – are actualized in three semantic components. This has significant implications for language pedagogy as, in planning a scheme of work or a session, language teachers can refer to these sociolinguistic fundamentals as foundations for their practice. This was the case during this particular research project and is illustrated in the table on the following page.

Another theorist who has greatly illuminated this research has been Cook (2000), who sees language play as central to learning, creativity and intellectual development. Language play leads to imaginary worlds, he writes, and the fictions it produces serve to help us find out more than we already know. In this sense, play can serve something which is *not* play and should not, therefore, be regarded as self indulgent or frivolous. 'Fiction which performs no immediate service is particularly useful, for by freeing the mind from obligation and constraint, it refreshes, rearranges, and provides the free play of ideas on which innovative thinking depends' (Cook, 2000, p. 42).

Such a perspective chimes readily with the Vygotskyan view of play as *mediational* – a social means through which learners co-construct learning resources which, in turn, shape their understanding and promote further development (1978). Playful activities thus enable learners to see things afresh and make new sense. As both fictional *and* playful, well planned drama activities can thus make learning of all kinds possible and can, at one and the same time, be both instrumental *and* liberating in their effects.

The following table is modified from Halliday's model used to demonstrate how a *text* is also a *situation type*. Here certain scenes in Macbeth have been used to illustrate the interface of semiotics and semantic dimensions of situations.

	SITUATIONAL	SEMANTIC	
Field	The ongoing activity Subject matter *Meeting supernatural beings* *Planning a murder*	Language as about something Content function *Three prophecies* *Gaining power*	**Ideational**
Tenor	The role relationships involved Levels of formality *Two comrades interact with three witches* *Interaction between a man and his wife, Macbeth and Lady Macbeth*	Language as doing something Participatory function *Questioner/respondent; doubter/informer* *Arguing, persuading, manipulating*	**Interpersonal**
Mode	The symbolic or rhetorical channel Medium *Alternating between dialogue and monologue* *Dialogue* *Pragmatic*	Language in relation to the environment (verbal and non-verbal) Enabling function *Conspiratorial* *Demanding a specific decision* *Coercion into a specific plan*	**Textual**

In the rest of this chapter, we outline a lesson structure influenced by this model and by the practice of the Royal Shakespeare Company's educational department (Royal Shakespeare Company, 2010). The unit of Macbeth is used as a practical example to illustrate what the scheme of work might look like and the implementation is discussed under four headings: contextualizing the play, negotiating meanings, staging and plenary reflections. Examples of how the students responded to individual activities can be found at the end of the chapter.

Contextualizing the play

There are several ways to start a session. Of central concern is that the students' attention and awareness be orientated to the play through the pedagogy. It might begin with enactment or with a game to suggest a theme or message. Both approaches involve active physical work. The purpose thus is two-fold: to make the play feel relevant and to set up an atmosphere in which drama and language can become the twin drivers to energise the class. Here are two examples:

1.   An enactment

Building an altar: Two desks and some objects (water bottles, books, candles etc.) are placed in the middle of the space. A volunteer is asked to read Lady Macbeth's soliloquy from Act 1, Scene 5 in which she reacts with stark ambition to a letter just received from her husband. The student is asked to play with the given objects as she reads and to begin to build something from them, a task that should be done intuitively. The class is asked to note how this process affects her reading and their responses are elicited when she has finished.

The raven himself is hoarse
That croaks the fatal entrance of Duncan
Under my battlement. Come, you spirits
That tend on mortal thoughts, unsex me here
And fill me from the crown to the toe top-full
Of direst cruelty. Make thick my blood,
Stop up th' access and passage to remorse,
You wait on nature's mischief. Come, thick night,
And pall thee in the dunnest smoke of hell,
That my keen knife see not the wound it makes,
Nor heaven peep through the blanket of the dark,
To cry 'Hold, hold!'

This activity can be used to explore such themes as ambition, greed and power as suggested through both the language and the manipulation of the semiotic signs, which here exemplify how cultural artefacts can take on a mediational function, helping students make sense of the text.

A note on dealing with challenging vocabulary

Throughout this project, students were always introduced to a new text by being asked first of all to read it around the class twice, from punctuation mark to punctuation mark.

They could then ask for the meanings of any words or phrases, which were explained to them through examples of sentences and phrases they could readily understand. During subsequent group activities, Astrid would make sure that each group could make sense of the lines they were working with. After groups had presented their work, she found that the rest of the class were almost always able to make sense of the words from the way that each group had imaged and performed them.

2. A purposeful game

Passing around the desire ball. Ask students to share with the class a dark desire that they perhaps want more than anything else in the world. This is done by passing around the ball. It is like a crystal ball; look into it and wish hard enough and it might even come true. Teachers can then playfully draw attention to the underlying messages revealed through their wishes. If appropriate, they can relate them to the characters or texts they are going to explore. On the surface, playing games such as this may relate only indirectly to the play but, liberated from obligation and constraint, students are being allowed to respond transgressively and thus see parts of themselves in perhaps the most unlikely characters. Thus a collective, free play of ideas can help them approach afresh the text under examination.

Negotiating meanings

After the space has been energized, the session can proceed to the main activities. The focus of the lesson will vary, of course, depending on the progression of the story and the learning needs of students. In the first session of a new scheme, the setting and characters might be the focus and, instead of reading the character list, you might have students act them out. Here is an example:

1. Still image of key themes or characters

Students walk around the space. On hearing the teacher's instruction, they are to make a still image, responding to that instruction, either individually or collaboratively. The still images include: friends celebrating/a king and his subjects/two people who don't trust each other/two people conspiring. They are encouraged to play on levels. Pick out one or two images that display interesting characteristics to comment on. Ask students to remember the images they have formed as they relate to the work they are about to do.

In some sessions language work might take up most of the time slot. It is important to bear in mind that drama strategies and language work should work in such a way that they complement one another dynamically. Active approaches to language are intended to engage students both physically and linguistically, allowing them to negotiate meanings by embodying language and physicalizing images. Here are five examples. The first is based on the extract from Lady Macbeth's monologue presented above.

2. Choreographing key words

   a. Ask students to identify from each line one key word that best captures its essence and then to come up with different ways to say that key word. Next, create a gesture to go with it.

b. Students now present their choreography to the whole class. Before the presentation, ask them to pay attention to the images they are going to see and the voice qualities they are going to hear. Afterwards, question them on specific images: What did you see? What did you hear? From these images, what do we now know about Lady Macbeth? What does she mean when she says 'unsex me'? and so on.

c. Draw students' attention to the lines *'pall thee in the dunnest smoke of hell'* and *'my keen knife see not the wound it makes'*. Ask what effects the personification creates as evoked by the relevant images they have just seen.

3. Imaging the word

Divide the class into groups. They are given three to four lines to work with from Act 5, Scene 5.

Tomorrow, and tomorrow, and tomorrow
Creeps in this petty pace from day to day
To the last syllable of recorded time;
And all our yesterdays have lighted fools
The way to dusty death. Out, out, brief candle!
Life's but a walking shadow, a poor player
That struts and frets his hour upon the stage
And then is heard no more. It is a tale
Told by an idiot, full of sound and fury,
Signifying nothing.

Students should come up with a gesture for each word. Invite the whole class to try this out by first of all imaging the opening two lines together. When students have presented their performances, draw attention to the overall image or picture of the section they have worked on. Ask questions like 'What were some of the images we saw?' 'What were this group's hand gestures like in relation to their bodies?' 'Did the performers present mostly high or low level pictures?' 'How does that inform their interpretation of the sentences?'

4. Texture of vowels

Ask students to pick out the vowels of the stressed syllables. If we take the same extract (Act 5, Scene 5) as an example, they will pick out o, i, e and so on. Contrast those with the short vowels in *'That struts and frets his hour upon the stage'*. This can lead to a discussion about how the lengthy, rounded vowels of the first lines suggest a sense of eternity that contrasts with the short, sharp vowel sounds that reflect the small and petty actions of one individual.

5. Changing directions

This activity is designed for the soliloquy in Act 1, Scene 7. The lines are as follows:

If it were done when 'tis done, then 'twere well
It were done quickly.
He's here in double trust:
First, as I am his kinsman and his subject,
Strong both against the deed; then, as his host,
Who should against his murderer shut the door,

Not bear the knife myself. Besides, this Duncan
Hath borne his faculties so meek, hath been
So clear in his great office, that his virtues
Will plead like angels trumpet-tongued against
The deep damnation of his taking-off,
I have no spur
To prick the sides of my intent, but only
Vaulting ambition, which o'erleaps itself
And falls on the other—

Students read the lines and turn in a different direction at each punctuation mark. When they finish the first reading, ask: how has the activity helped them with their understanding? Have they noticed places where they have to change directions very often? What does this suggest? Point to how the first two lines feature only words of one syllable. What feelings does this suggest to them when they read out loud? Students are then asked to read the lines again, bearing these questions in mind.

6. Running to different corners

    The class is divided into two groups. One group sits at the side watching while the members of the other group spread themselves around the space. Those in the space are to read the lines until they hear the teacher call out the word 'run', upon which they are to run to a corner and continue the lines from there. This is repeated several times until the soliloquy is finished. At the end, the players will be spread around different corners of the room. Elicit responses from both the audience and the players.

Students usually find difficulty comprehending the meanings of Shakespearean lines. If we approach purely through literal and grammatical means, the difficulty is understandable. Cicely Berry, the voice director for the Royal Shakespeare Company, asks actors to resist the inclination of the 'over-educated response', and play with their language instinct. The unity of speech and physical movement that underpins her exercises for actors is transferable to a drama classroom as the work that actors do can also be used to make the heightened text and extravagant images accessible to students.

Berry states that the principle behind these exercises is to bring out the 'tactile nature of the sound' (1993, p. 104). To speak out the words while the body is in movement – running, jumping, pushing, pulling – can release the energies they contain. Some movements may seem absurd, in the sense that they do not correspond to grammatical meanings, but it is this very absurdity that liberates students from the need to make literal sense. The movements work poetically, helping students discover different possibilities for meaning through the rhythms, sounds and very texture of the words. As Berry puts it: 'we have to find ways to get them not only on our tongue, but to make them part of our whole physical self in order to release them from the tyranny of the mind' (1993, p. 22).

In addition to their textures of sound and variations of rhythm, Shakespearean lines provoke meanings through images that Berry believes express some need or self image of the character who speaks them:

From an actor's point of view the images are of two kinds: those which paint an external picture, and those revealing an inner landscape ... they are always an extension of the character, of how he perceives things.

(Berry, 1993, p. 111)

The lines are packed full of actions and simply speaking them cannot pin these down; instead, it makes them descriptive. Their physical force and energy is what brings alive the character's state of mind and mindset. Physicalizing the lines, not literally but in a manner that grasps the spirit of the pictures they paint, can serve to illuminate the interplay between imagery and intention.

The exercises mentioned above are just a few examples adapted from those presented in *The Actor and The Text*. Central is the need to release language from 'the tyranny of mind' (1993, p. 22). In Berry's words, feeling the energy of a text in your body will hopefully draw out the delight and spontaneity in the language (2008, p. 36). These exercises are liberating through the opportunities they offer for playing with the basic units of lines, their rhythm and metre, their combination of vowels and consonants. The apparent absurdity is highly practical in a way that works against reductive impulses of rationality; it helps actors find a personalized connection to the text. It is also meant to be highly enjoyable:

> it is just so good to feel your whole body become part of the words you speak – they just begin to take on a different texture. And because it is slightly ridiculous, you are free to enjoy the language.
>
> (Berry, 1993, p. 187)

Productive absurdity such as this, moreover, can release the pleasure in learning language. It is no accident that Berry's paradoxical approach – so successful with generations of Shakespearean actors – echoes closely Cook's theory of language play, referred to in the introductory section of this chapter.

If pun or irony is implied in the text, it is worth exploring with students as mental processes of 'reading between the lines' can then be made visual through enactment. The ways characters speak the lines, their facial expressions and positions in relation to each other can work together to enhance and highlight ironic effects.

7. Choral speaking

Divide the class into three groups and give each a line from Act 1, Scene 5. The lines are: *Bear welcome in your eye, Your hand, your tongu e/Look like th' innocent flower, But be the serpent under' t/He that's coming must be provided for.* As the students are forming the still images, they should take into consideration the characters, the action and the tone the passage suggests. Who might be involved? Who should be provided with what? How can they juxtapose a flower and a serpent? Students are to present their lines as they form their images. Conventionally, 'provide' means 'support' or 'take care of'. What kind of message is Lady Macbeth trying to convey? By using *provided for* in this context, what kind of identity is she creating for herself? How does the stark contrast between flower and serpent underline this? Physicalizing these lines makes explicit the irony and demonstrates how language can be used actively (and in this case viciously) to construct and assert an identity.

Several drama conventions can help explore character relationships as expressed through language. *Thought tracking* provides a 'safe' frame that invites students to express their personal thoughts in a public space. Voicing for a character can protect students who are uncomfortable with standing out in front of others, while still giving them the opportunity to practise the language and contribute their thoughts to the class. *Sculpting characters* and positioning them in relation to each other can be done before thought-tracking. An interesting example is the relationship between Macbeth and Banquo after they have heard the prophecies of the witches.

8.   Sculpting characters

The class sits in a circle. Invite two volunteers into the circle and ask the rest to sculpt them into possible images of Macbeth and Banquo directly after the scene with the witches. Ask: what might each be thinking in response to the prophecy? How might it have affected their attitude towards each other? Invite students to thought-track each of them in turn before telling them that a messenger now arrives with the news that the Thane of Cawdor has betrayed Scotland and that the king is rewarding Macbeth by granting him his title. Ask students to change the images of Macbeth and Banquo to reflect their responses to one another upon receiving this news, which points to the accuracy of the witches' prophecies.

Students' comments can be incorporated into subsequent sessions, when appropriate, and can even be transformed into an activity, an exercise that can have an empowering effect as it demonstrates that you value their responses. After working on Lady Macbeth's plan for the night of King Duncan's arrival, for example, one of the students used the Chinese idiom 千頭萬緒 to describe Macbeth's reaction. The idiom consists of four characters. The word for word translation is as follows:

千 thousand

頭 head

萬 ten thousand

緒 threads

This idiom resonates with the state of mind Macbeth experiences in the soliloquy from Act 1, Scene 7 quoted above. An activity was thus devised, inspired by the metaphoric nature of this Chinese idiom, one that can be readily adapted to explore such emotions as hesitation, disturbance, and confusion.

9.   Web of thoughts

Divide the class into two groups, A and B. Ask one volunteer from group A to read the soliloquy. The rest of group A are to position themselves in the space, imagining that they are inside Macbeth's head. Group B is the audience. The volunteer is given a ball of thread wrapped around a dagger. As the volunteer reads the lines, she has to bring the thread to one person and continue to another each time she reaches a punctuation mark. She can change direction whenever she feels it appropriate. The result is that, by the end of the soliloquy, the thread is completely entangled. How can this be understood as an image of what is going on in Macbeth's mind? Ask students to write down any phrases that capture the essence of the image they have seen enacted here.

In a sociocultural approach to SLA, teachers should take into account the social context of students. Social context does not just mean the classroom setting, but also the world outside the classroom which can present resources to channel learning for particular groups of students. Idioms or metaphors are culturally constructed artefacts which can be used as mediational means to enhance understanding of L2, rather than to be avoided as too difficult or obscure.

Staging

Shakespeare gives very few explicit instructions as stage directions. The setting is usually suggested through the characters' lines. This yields great opportunities for challenging students to find clues to the setting through close reading of the text. Smells, aural effects, visual signs and textural feelings abound and can be brought to life when we dramatize the scene. When King Duncan is murdered, for example, characters constantly refer to the night, and it is worthwhile having students experience the atmosphere.

Creating a soundtrack

Distribute the edited lines below, spoken by Lennox in Act 2, Scene 3. Ask students to underline words that suggest aural effects and to pick out words that add qualities to the sounds. Then split the class into three groups and divide the lines between them. The responsibility of each team is to create a soundscape for their given lines. One volunteer is to stand in the middle of the space with the other students surrounding her. She then reads the lines accompanied by the sound effects. The sounds are pieced together by the teacher as she cues in different groups. A 'script' for this might look as follows:

> The night has been <u>unruly</u>. Where we lay,
> Our chimneys were <u>blown</u> down, and, as they say,
> <u>Lamentings heard</u> in the air, strange <u>screams</u> of death,
> And <u>prophesying</u> with <u>accents</u> terrible
> The obscure <u>bird</u>
> <u>Clamoured</u> the livelong night. Some <u>say</u>, the earth
> Was feverous and did shake.

Plenary reflections

After students have studied key characters and conflicts of the play, it might be useful to have a plenary activity in order to draw out individual responses and encourage debate. This is an opportunity for the whole class to make sense of what they have learned and to negotiate interpretations. One effective way of doing this is through a strategy known as *silent argument*, which tracks the progression of a written discussion and offers a secure mode for quiet students. This activity also frames the discussion as an exploratory process rather than an explanatory one. Another helpful activity is *stream of consciousness*. The subsequent talk that ensues from this kind of writing ensures that students' personal reflections are brought into the public and social domain.

1. Silent argument

    Lay down a long strip of paper in the space. Invite students to write down their reflections on the scene when Macbeth finds out about Lady Macbeth's death. They can do this by jotting down a question or a comment. They can also respond to anyone else's comments or questions by writing on that same piece of paper. After the argument is finished, invite students to walk around the paper and stand next to a comment that has particularly struck them and then to read it out loud.

2. Stream of consciousness

After exploring key scenes in a session, students find a space for themselves. Tell them that this exercise is not collaborative and ask them to write down or draw whatever comes to their minds with regard to the text. Then invite them to read one sentence from their writing to the whole class.

The purpose of reflective work such as this is to use the target language to invite and investigate. Language is being used not to explain but to raise awareness and challenge perceptions. And it is their own language that does this. If the solitary part of the activities prepares them for the public discussion, the collective part promotes learning through social interaction and oral participation. In these activities, we have found that students often use question and answer sequences and repair sequences characteristic of private speech. As Vygostsky has informed us, private speech has social origins. In the process of privatizing speech, higher forms of mental function arise on the *intrapsychological* plane. The reflective discussions then provide an *interpsychological* plane for private speech to evolve into inner speech (Vygotsky, 1978)

Students' responses

After each session, students were asked to write their responses in their own personal journals, in English and/or Chinese, as they wished. Most chose to write entirely in English and the extracts below are presented as written, although the names of the contributors have been changed.

■ On thought-tracking

Wen-Yi: *We can take part in what we are learning, such as acting out the scenes and discuss the characters' tones when speaking.*
Ling: *I have enjoyed the way we played with our 'bodies' – positions, levels, etc. And I do believe that these practices help me understand the play more.*

■ On choreographing key words

Han-Ting: *We not only showed the meanings, but also the symbols. Although each group got only three words, it gave me the impression of the whole story.*
Lin-Lo: *The performance of the first group was splendid! Posture of 'Raven' interpreted 'fatal entrance' so vividly, which inspired me a lot. I think this is how the activity should work, full of charm and creativity. Through this kind of course, I think I understand details in Macbeth well.*
Na-Na: *To create gestures for each important word helps us think beyond the lines and makes the line itself more expressive.*
Pei-Ling: *When we were doing 'Raven', I felt quite ... scared and upset. It seemed that all the things were dead, and the air was heavy. That was a strange feeling because we were just acting out something. But it can make sense of ... horror.*

Shu-Yu: ... *it makes words come alive. It's pretty hard to describe, so all I can say is that it gives substance to words that have meanings which are hard to understand. The most memorable action and key word for me is 'unsex', as the word is initially difficult to understand, but when paired with an action, it is easy to see what the word means and why Shakespeare chose to use that word in that particular context.*

Mei-Shan: *As our group started to figure out what Shakespeare wanted to deliver, we found many possibilities ... the discussion revealed the subtle hints behind the sentences. I had lots of fun. I enjoyed digging into the world of language, although sometimes it's a bit too exquisite to understand.*

■ On running to the corner

Ting-An: *It's very clear this time that every bizarre activity we did is to concretize those abstract things under the sentences. I like the first group. They ran rapidly to show Macbeth's changing thought. That made me think of one dance of* 雲門舞集 [Cloud Gate Dance Theatre]. *The dancers also walked quickly from corner to corner.*

Rong-Hui: *I think in this way we can feel how Macbeth felt. It helped us to get to the nervous, anxious and self-contradictory emotions when he was making the decision.*

■ On changing directions

(This is actually a transcription from the session, not a journal extract)
A-Lin: *He is not sure what to do ... reasoning with himself?*
Lia: *He is nervous, like we walk to and fro in the room before exams.*
Pei-Yu: *He keeps changing his mind.*
...
Teacher: [After the second reading of Macbeth's soliloquy of Act 1 Scene 7] *What about the first two lines? What did you feel like or sound like when you read them?*
Ya-Wen: *I had to gasp.*
Teacher: *Gasping? Like after you ran from the third floor to the tenth floor for my class? (General laughter)*
Ya-Wen: *(Laughing) No ... don't know.*
Wei: *Lia said it's like he was nervous.*

■ On web of thoughts

Kai: *When I was acting Macbeth, I didn't know I would walk that way – obviously walking in a circle. I think it may also be the illustration of Macbeth's fluctuating mind.*

Ying-Nien: *If the string was long enough, the shape we made might have seem a ball of yarn ... it intended to show the disorder in his mind.*

■ On building an altar

Shu-Yu: *I personally think it is very creepy, because it felt like I was getting ready to sacrifice something ... it really did help me get in character*

Wan-Ron: *In the beginning I was confused, but I found it surprising as the emotions were built up by piling stuff.*

Li-Ya: *Li-Wen (one of the girls who played Lady Macbeth) is really getting aggressive and ambitious! It's cool that acting can do this to us.*

Ting: *It seems that I'm a little bit lacking in imagination because I can barely convince myself that the table is an altar and the box is not just a box. It can be anything you want when you are imagining building an altar. Sometimes we are just confined to the shape, the exterior of the object and it's difficult to envision it is another thing whereas I still had lots of fun when I played Lady Macbeth.*

■ On creating soundtracks

Shui-Xien: *The sound effect gave me a strong impression on the murder. It really gave me goose bumps.*
Ai: *As we were making sounds, we needed to concentrate on the play more carefully than usual.*
Ling: *The tension of the scene became more and more intense. It was like the stage was cursed. And I think the whole class cooperated perfectly, with the creepy footsteps and bird chirps. Everything pulled out scarily and theatrically.*

■ On silent argument

Yan-Hui: *It was fun because it developed into some sort of chatting while kind of discussed the scenes. I didn't imagine the play was a bit like* 紅樓夢 [Dreams of the Red Chamber] *until a classmate pointed it out.*
Ching: *Everyone can write whatever she wants to say! We can argue silently. I feel safer like this. I am not afraid of responding to questions.*
Wen-Lun: *It's great that we can also learn something from other's opinion and viewpoint of Macbeth!*

Conclusion

This work has been positioned within the social orientation of SLA, in the belief that to assume a dichotomy between the social and the cognitive would be neither necessary nor useful. Drama pedagogy which values and promotes participation, interaction and collaboration can create learning opportunities to engage students through language, physicality and other mediational means. Language development takes place through the on-going contact of the mind with the here-and-now idiosyncrasies of the environment. In this sense, the learning process is dynamic. In van Geert's words, it is 'embodied and embedded action' (2008, p. 184). In a course where language is the object of study and the major means of instruction, drama pedagogy aptly brings out the dialogic nature of language and makes use of embodied and embedded ways of learning.

References

Berry, C. (1993). *The actor and the text* (rev. ed.). London: Virgin Books.
Berry, C. (2008). *From word to play: A handbook for directors*. London: Oberon Books.
Cook, G.W.D. (2000). *Language play, language learning*. Oxford: Oxford University Press.
Firth, A., & Wagner, J. (1997). On discourse, communication, and (some) fundamental concepts in SLA research. *The Modern Language Journal, 81*(3), 285–300.
Freeman, D.L., & Cameron, L. (2008). Research methodology on language development from a complex systems perspective. *The Modern Language Journal, 92*(2), 200–213.
van Geert, P. (2008). The dynamic systems approach in the study of L1 and L2 acquisition: An introduction. *The Modern Language Journal, 92*(2), 179–199.
Halliday, M.A.K. (1978). *Language as social semiotic*. London: Arnold.
Lantolf, J.P. (2000). *Sociocultural theory and second language learning*. Oxford: Oxford University Press.
Royal Shakespeare Company (2010). *The RSC Shakespeare toolkit for teachers*. London: Methuen Drama.
Vygotsky, L.S. (1978). *Mind in society: The development of higher psychological processes*. Cambridge, MA: Harvard University Press.

Digital Storytelling, Drama and Second Language Learning

Kirsty McGeoch

Digital stories are created by weaving together images, music and voice-over narrations into engaging two- to three-minute movies. This chapter starts with a brief introduction to digital storytelling, its place in second language learning and how drama might support both the development of digital stories and language. It then describes the steps taken to develop digital stories in the second language classroom, highlighting how drama games and conventions can be used to enhance this process. Although my own work has been in the field of young adult education, the process as described here is directly applicable to secondary classrooms. I present it as a model that can be readily adapted for students with English as an Additional Language or in the context of second language classrooms in which students are engaged in intermediate or advanced studies.

Digital storytelling

Digital storytelling was pioneered by the Center for Digital Storytelling (CDS) in California, whose model and workshop methodology are underpinned by the following assumptions:

- Everyone has a story to tell.

- Voice is nurtured through careful listening.

- Creativity is human activity.

- Technology offers 'inexhaustible potential' for creative expression.

- People perceive the world in different ways and so 'good' stories can take many different shapes.

(CDS, date unspecified)

While noting that there is no strict formula, the CDS has distilled the structure and design of digital stories into the following seven elements: (Lambert, 2002, pp. 45–59).

1.   Point (of view): the author must define the point of the story.

2.   Dramatic question: does the story set up some tension that is later resolved?

3.   Emotional content: truthful stories that deal with themes of love, loss, death, confidence, vulnerability, acceptance and rejection improve the likelihood of holding the audience's attention.

4.   The gift of your voice: recording a natural-sounding voice-over. The teller's voice is unique and conveys its own special meaning.

5.   The power of soundtrack: choosing music which complements or adds an extra layer of meaning.

6.   Economy: being selective with the script, editing out text which may be conveyed through images. The general guideline is about 250–300 words, which translates into a three minute story.

7.   Pacing: the rhythm of the story is crucial in sustaining the interest of the audience.

Digital storytelling and second language learning

In making the case for digital storytelling in second language learning, and for a later positioning of drama within that, I draw primarily on the work of Leo van Lier (1996, 2004), whose ecological approach is at once a theory of language and of learning. An ecological approach regards language and learning as dialogic and occurring through social interaction. It is a view that not only sees language and culture as mutually constitutive, but also foregrounds the important relationship between self, identity, voice, agency, motivation and language learning. In line with such a perspective, digital storytelling can be seen to support second language learning in a number of ways.

Digital storytelling and classroom interaction

In contrast to the initiation-response-feedback pattern of talk that is pervasive in classrooms, the process of creating a digital story prompts different kinds of interaction. For example, the whole-class workshopping of each student's story and later peer review both involve a great deal of contingent communication as the teacher and students ask each other genuine questions for which they do not yet know the answers.

Digital storytelling and the intercultural dimension of language learning

An ecological approach focuses on language 'as relations between people and the world, and on language learning as ways of relating more effectively to people and the world' (van Lier, 2004, p. 4). Central to the effectiveness of such relating is the development of intercultural competence. According to Scarino and Liddicoat (2009), being intercultural 'involves much more than just knowing about another culture: it involves learning how one's own culture shapes perceptions of oneself, of the world and our relationship to others' (p. 21). Thus, *intra*cultural awareness is foundational to the intercultural.

As personal narratives are strong forms of self-identification, which can serve as windows into our beliefs, values and culture (Bruner, 1994), it follows that composing, sharing, shaping and reflecting on the stories we tell about ourselves, and those of others, would have the potential to foster both intracultural and intercultural awareness. The following comments are indicative of such understandings.

> *Before starting, I thought a lot to seek something that I want to share. The more I did, the clearer I saw myself. I realized what is important for me and what I treasure most, as well as what I should do in the following few years.*

> (Fan, China)

> *I think that participating in this digital storytelling exchange helped me to empathy with classmate's feeling.*

> (Sun-Young, Korea)

Digital storytelling, group dynamics and community

The sharing of personal stories has the potential to create a strong sense of community in the classroom.

> *I really feel like we are a family, to do the whole thing and show each other our own story – it make each other feel warm.*

> (Fan, China)

Such a feeling of community is significant as supportive classroom atmospheres and group dynamics are seen as positively linked to learning (Dörnyei & Murphey, 2003; Senior, 2002) and are important dimensions of pedagogical scaffolding within the ZPD (van Lier, 2007).

Digital stories as identity texts

Of primary significance to language learning is the development of the learner's identity and voice in the target language (van Lier, 1996, 2004). These are related in important ways to learner agency, motivation and investment in the learning process, as well as to achievement.

While my research and subsequent projects did not set out to measure gains in language proficiency, students have consistently reported improvements in their English, particularly in terms of pronunciation, speaking and writing. These perceived improvements may be linked to the desire to create a quality end-product, which in turn prompts students to spend hours practising, revising and refining their work. This level of investment may be explained by the fact that digital stories are about the tellers' lives, an expression of who they are, and as such can be described as 'identity texts'; texts which can 'hold a mirror up to students in which their identities are reflected back in a positive light' (Cummins, 2006, p. 60). When such texts are shared with multiple audiences, they are likely to generate positive responses and affirm the creators (Chow & Cummins, 2003, cited in Cummins, 2006, p. 60). Technology can further amplify levels of identity investment and positive feedback by making texts look more accomplished.

For Cummins (2006), identity investment is a vital component of deep learning and '*the negotiation of identities* is a primary determinant of whether or not students will engage cognitively in the learning process' (p. 53). The high levels of investment and intrinsic motivation demonstrated by students making digital stories are reflected in the comment below:

> I do not consider it just a project, as a course to gain some marks. I want to do it from the bottom of my heart.

(Fan, China)

Digital storytelling and multimodality

Digital stories are multimodal texts, conveying meaning through a complex inter-weaving of image, music and spoken word, and thereby opening up more communica-tive possibilities for authors to reach their audiences. This is particularly significant for second language learners as it affords them opportunities to express themselves beyond what they may be capable of linguistically (Nelson, 2006). When combined with explicit teaching of the multiliteracies (New London Group, 2000), the process of making digital stories can also build students' multimodal communicative competence (Royce, 2002) or semiotic competence (van Lier, 2007) and further amplify their authorial intent.

Digital storytelling and the aesthetic dimension of language

Crafting digital stories is a creative process that puts students in touch with the aesthetic dimensions of language and other semiotic modes. Abbs (1989) suggests that students engage in the aesthetic dimension of language when they draw on different literary genres (including autobiography) to create their own intertextual artefacts to be per-formed or shared with an audience.

For van Lier (1998) creative language use is also a form of intuitive language awareness, and as Carter (2007) notes, something that allows learners to express their identities more fully. As digital storytelling gives rise to self-expression and creative language use, it can therefore support second language learning in impor-tant ways.

Prelude to the digital storytelling course and a case for including drama

In adapting the basic format developed by the Center for Digital Storytelling for the context of second language learning, I felt that the process of both engaging more deeply with narrative and supporting L2 development could be further enhanced by embedding a variety of creative arts activities, particularly drama.

In establishing a rationale for incorporating drama, it is important to note that drama has been found to support language learning in many of the ways described earlier in relation to digital storytelling.

■ Drama gives contexts for using language in meaningful ways (Liu, 2002), provides opportunities to experiment with a range of registers and genres (Ewing & Simons, 2004) and is often characterized by contingent, dialogical classroom interaction (Wolfe & Alexander, 2008).

■ Drama activities can also be harnessed in the service of intercultural education. Improvisational activities and being 'in role', can help people 'decentre' and see themselves and others in new lights, thereby developing empathy (Fleming, 2006, p. 61).

■ Drama is social and cooperative in nature and promotes a positive group dynamic and class atmosphere. It helps free students of their inhibitions so they feel able to take risks (Hughes, 1993; Liu, 2002).

■ Drama may assist in the formation of second language identities as it allows students to experiment with different social roles behind the safety of a mask. Such roles can sometimes form the basis of the public styles students later assume in class (Dörnyei & Malderez, 1997, p. 77).

■ Drama is a multimodal pedagogy which is effective in supporting language learning and can offer teachers innovative ways of validating the experiences, cultures and literacy practices of their students (Norton, 2010).

■ Drama engages students in the aesthetic dimension of language learning (Marschke, 2005). Further, Sullivan (2000, cited in Ellis, 2003, p. 190) has found that 'fun' and playfulness while performing activities such as role plays serve to mediate the learning process and can enhance receptivity to language learning.

Practical overview of how digital storytelling and drama work in the classroom

This section provides a practical overview of the ten steps involved in making digital stories and how drama activities can be incorporated into this process. The course described here typically takes between twenty-five to thirty hours of teaching.

Step one – Building trust, group feeling and orientating the class to the project

Initially, as with any language class, it is important to establish rapport and start building trust. Having a supportive class atmosphere is not only conducive to second language learning but is essential in terms of creating the affective space necessary for digital stories to be authored. As the day I start a digital storytelling project is usually my first class with any given group, I usually break the ice with a short drama game for everyone to get to know each other's names.

FIGURE 10.1 Open with a name game

Drama name and gesture game

This involves each student giving his/her name accompanied by a physical gesture and starts with the group standing in a circle. I like dancing so I often do a flamenco-style move or twirl of some kind. The whole class repeats my name and gesture three times and then we move on to the next person, who gives his/her name and gesture. The whole class then repeats all the names and gestures from the top (mine). Once the circle is complete, the game begins. I say my name and give my gesture and then the name and gesture of one of the participants. That participant then gives her/his name and gesture and that of another class member and so on. The game gets progressively faster, and students are eliminated if they forget someone's name or gesture, until there is a winning pair at the end.

Some students give bold and dramatic gestures, others give understated ones. What they are essentially giving is a first glimpse of their personality. It is an activity that never fails to generate a lot of laughter, and we all get to know each other's names ; something that has been shown to greatly affect group dynamics and classroom atmosphere (Dörnyei & Murphey, 2003).

After this game, I welcome the students more officially and tell them that as our project involves telling our stories, it is important to get to know each other better. As part of this process, I explain that we will be doing some drama, speaking and writing activities, and gather their general consensus for this. From there I move to the first of the process-drama techniques known as teacher-in-role and enactment of the expert.

Teacher-in-role involves students working with the teacher within the drama. It provides 'a chance for students and teacher to lay aside their actual roles and take on role relationships which have a variety of status and power variables' (Neelands, 1990, p. 32). For example, if the class is creating a scene from the Titanic, the teacher may assume the role of the ship's captain. The idea is not to 'act' for the student audience (Morgan & Saxton, 1987), but to adopt a suitable role in order to create interest, increase tension, manage the action, develop the narrative and so on (Neelands, 1990).

Enactment of the expert, as developed by Hughes and Arnold (2008), is inspired by Dorothy Heathcote's concept of mantle of the expert (Heathcote & Bolton, 1994) in which 'The group become characters endowed with specialist knowledge that is relevant to the situation ... the situation is usually task-oriented ... power and responsibility move from teacher to group; learners feel respected by having expert status' (Neelands, 1990, p. 23).

With the students enrolled as experts, the teacher typically assumes a less powerful role and appeals to them for their assistance.

Enactment of the expert has been acknowledged as a covert way of allowing students to re-assess their 'sense of agency, competency and mastery' (Arnold, 2005, p. 42) by engaging in tasks in which they are likely to be successful. This is particularly important in second-language contexts where learners often find their self-concepts as competent communicators dramatically challenged.

There are three cycles in enactment of the expert: teacher planning, the active experience together with exploration of the text or problem and, finally, student and teacher reflections (Hughes & Arnold, 2008).

Cycle 1: Planning

The teacher's first task is to select a text or problem for students to explore, one which can provide the opportunity for the students to develop understandings in advance of what would normally be possible at their stage of development. The teacher also needs to decide what type of expert she/he wishes to encourage the students to experience. It is crucial that the students are encouraged to adopt a role with which they are familiar and that this role be of high status. The teacher can then plan the stages of the process and may prepare certain scripts. However, since the approach is student-centred and interactive, there will be a need to improvise and adapt throughout the experience.

Cycle 2: The enactment experience

This cycle includes four stages: developing the affective space (Hughes & Johnson, 1998), development of role, exploration of the text/completion of challenge and presentation of the findings.

Cycle 3: Reflection

The final cycle involves debriefing the role experience and a range of reflective experiences can be undertaken, such as writing in role, writing to one's peers or an absent classmate, preparing visual images of the experience and/or preparing an academic oral or written report.

In my two research cycles, I had students enroll as leading cultural anthropologists and as English language professors from the world's most prestigious universities, respectively (McGeoch & Hughes, 2009). Since then, I have used enactment of the expert to enroll students as film makers from the top studios in the world. Being familiar with movies, most students have found it an easy role to adopt. Pre-existing knowledge of story and film conventions can then be tapped in order to interpret the text – a digital story – and in discussing the various meta aspects of the genre at different stages throughout the course. Rather than having students explore and develop strong roles in a fictional world, enactment of the expert is used here as a tool for building the group dynamic and for examining the different aspects of the genre of digital storytelling in an engaging way. As the 'experts' are called upon at different times over a series of lessons, reflection on the drama experience (Cycle 3) has tended to come at the end of the course.

Here in *Step one*, we will see examples of the different stages of Cycle 2 – building affective space, development of role, exploration of the text/completion of challenge and presentation of the findings. Some of these stages, namely completion of a challenge and presentation of findings, will also reappear in subsequent steps of the digital storytelling process.

Building the affective space

Ok everyone, let's stand up and walk around the space ... don't look at anyone in particular ... just walk ... any direction is OK. Now as you walk, start making eye contact with others ... then smile ... walk, walk ... now greet each other ...

'Hi Kirsty'... keep walking. Now find a special spot in the room... a spot you feel comfortable in ... stop there ... that's your special spot ... now start walking again. As you walk, I want you to think of something that you are good at, something you really enjoy and are passionate about, something you are skilled at. (It can't be sleeping or watching TV!) Have you got the image in your mind? When I say FREEZE I want you to go to your special spot, close your eyes and freeze in the position of doing the thing you are good at ... 5 – 4 – 3 – 2 – 1 – FREEZE. Stay there now, keep your eyes closed and exaggerate the movement. Make it ten times bigger. Now, open your eyes. Turn to the person closest to you, show each other your statues and find out as much as possible about what you are both good at. Ask as many questions as you can, for example, 'How long have you been doing X? Why do you enjoy it so much? What got you interested in this? Have you ever won an award/ a competition for X?'

NOTE: This activity requires a large area to be made in the middle of the classroom so that students can move around. If such space is simply not available, then skip straight to the frozen statues as this can be done from behind a desk. Usually this part involves the students depicting something in which they have expertise. I usually expand that to include activities students are passionate about or enjoy, as it can be culturally awkward for some students to portray themselves as being 'good at' something. This activity can also be adapted for lower level groups by brainstorming questions about hobbies and special skills and looking at possible question forms before the activity.

Development of role

After the students have talked about their special skills, I ask them to close their eyes again, briefly resume their positions and remember how it feels to do the thing they are good at or enjoy. They can then take this feeling into the next activity in which they build roles as expert film makers. To set this activity up, I have the students sit at tables in small groups. I then put up a PowerPoint slide (or overhead transparency) welcoming them to the 1st International Film Makers Conference, in role as a conference organiser.

FIGURE 10.2 Introducing an expert role

Welcome everyone to the 1st International Film Makers Symposium to be held here in [insert the city/town/ village you are in]. *I am so excited to see here representatives from the top film studios in the world. It's just amazing. Thank you all so much for coming. Now we have a very exciting programme for you over the next couple of days, but before I talk about that, there is someone who has a special announcement to make.*

I then put on a hat or different jacket, and address them in role as Annie.

Hi everyone – my name is Annie and I am a student of film and a junior reporter for the Magic of Movies Show – the sponsor of this conference. I have to say I am feeling a bit star struck by all the big names in this room. Your work is truly an inspiration. Today, I am here to announce something exciting to start the conference. The Magic of Movies Show is running a competition to name the best film studio in the world. The prize? Twenty million dollars towards the production of your next feature film. That's 20 million dollars. There will also be a huge celebration for the winner – a cruise on Sydney Harbour, with fireworks and special guests, U2. I'll leave all the details with Kirsty and I'll come back in 45 minutes with the crew to film your pitches. Before I go, though, can you please write down the names of your film studios on the piece of paper in front of you and I'll come by and collect it in 1 minute on my way out. [Students to invent original names.]

Annie then reads out the list of film studios to the group and leaves the room, wishing them luck.

Out-of-role, I show the next slide giving them the details they need to include in their pitches:

OK guys – Annie has just given me the details of the competition. Now here's what you need to do before she comes back.

FIGURE 10.3 Developing roles as expert film makers

When Annie returns with the 'film crew', each studio presents its pitch, which invariably sparks a lot of laughter. They often come up with amusing studio names, like 'The Warner Sisters', draw very creative and elaborate maps and invent crazy awards; one studio won an Oscar for best animal actor in 'Kung-Fu Koala'.

Exploration of the text

FIGURE 10.4 Students will present their findings in role as experts

Back in role as conference organiser, I introduce the challenge.

Good morning, everyone and welcome back to day two of the symposium. What a night we had last night! As you know, our Sponsor decided that you were all equally deserving of the prize and so everyone partied on the harbour until the wee hours. Now before we get started with today's programme, I have a special request for you from Annie. She just sent me through the following email:

Subject:	Special request for the film makers.
Insert:	📎 Attachments 🖼 Photos ▾ ⊙ From Bing ▾ 😊 Emoticons
Tahoma ▾	10 ▾ **B** *I* <u>U</u> ▉ ▉ ▉ ▤ ▤ ▊ ▊ 🐛 ▱ **A**

Dear Kirsty,

How are you this morning? I am writing to see if you could ask the film makers a HUGE favour for me. For today's show, I have been preparing a short segment on new trends in film and just heard about something called digital storytelling. I managed to find an example of one, but it seems that the file is damaged and there is no audio. I am starting to panic as we are going to air very soon. I have attached the file and was hoping the film makers could look at it for me and tell me what they think it is about.

Thank you in advance for your assistance.

Kind regards,

Annie Johnstone

Junior reporter, The Magic of Movies Show

FIGURE 10.5 An e-mail request from the teacher in role

At this point we watch my digital story with the volume muted.

Presentation of the findings

The film makers discuss what they have seen and report back with their interpretations. Annie then sends through the complete version and we watch that to check their predictions.

Step 2 – Examining the elements of digital stories

While still in role, the film makers receive another request from Annie, this time related to the elements of digital storytelling. The film makers discuss these and give their suggestions.

> **Text message 97(1)**   abc
>
> **To**
>
> Btw can u pls ask the film makers
> about these? They are apparently
> the elements of digital stories but i
> am not sure what they mean???
>
> **Point of the story**
> **Dramatic Question**
> **Emotional Content**
> **The Gift of Your Voice**
> **The Power of Soundtrack**
> **Economy**
> **Pacing**
> **Thnx**
> **Annie**
>
> **Options**   **Close**

FIGURE 10.6 Being in role helps students examine the key elements of digital story making

Out of role, some time is spent discussing these elements and narrative features in general. Part of this involves having the students draw the typical 'shape' or map of a story and then introducing the concept of the 'story core': problem, resolution, change/realization (Ohler, 2008). I also encourage the students to consider whether stories are told differently in their cultures.

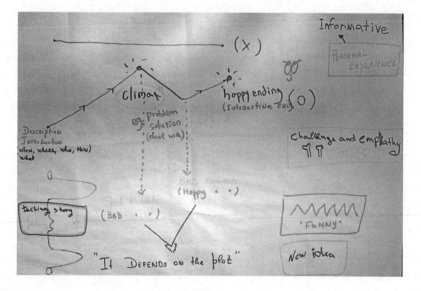

FIGURE 10.7 Students map the key elements of stories

During a recent digital storytelling course, I also invited a professional storyteller to the class and together we played the following storytelling/drama game:

All the people who ...

This is a version of the popular game 'fruit basket', in which chairs are set up in a circle, with one less chair than the total number of players and one person standing in the middle. The person in the middle throws down the first challenge: All the people who *have ever got lost* change chairs now. People who have been lost must stand up and find another chair to sit in. The person left standing has to tell the group the story of the time they got lost. The audience then asks for extra information they would like to know about the characters, setting and events, and gives feedback on different aspects of the storytelling performance, including: voice, animation, gestures, use of direct speech and the inclusion of vivid details. The process is then repeated by the next person standing in the middle with a new prompt.

Step 3 – Coming up with a story

Arguably the most challenging aspect of the project for students is unearthing their initial story idea. Viewing past digital stories can begin to trigger memories, as can discussions based on story prompts about turning points in their lives, their careers, their passions or influential people, for example. Free writing on these topics is another effective strategy, as is having students bring in special objects or photographs to talk about. Whatever the idea, the key to a good story is to show the personal significance of the given event, decision, relationship or object, rather than recounting a shopping list of 'things that happened'.

Step 4 – The story circle

The story circle is part of the Center for Digital Storytelling (CDS) workshop model and is considered to be a pivotal stage in the process. Seated in the circle, the students take turns reading out their first drafts, or sharing the ideas in their heads (as is more often the case). The rest of the group listens attentively and then gives supportive feedback. In my experience, the story circle has helped students to test out their initial script ideas to see if they are potentially engaging and also to find the focus of their stories. It is an activity which inspires the group to trust each other and has the effect of bonding the class as well. Before starting, students are reminded that they should only share what they feel comfortable and willing to share; that personal does not necessarily mean deeply private or confessional. From what I have observed, students seem to have a sense of their own boundaries.

Step 5 – Script development

Students continue to refine their scripts through a process of writing multiple drafts with the goal of honing them to fit within the 300-word limit. They share their writing with their peers and also review it in response to my feedback, either via email or over a class blog. This aspect of the project is certainly demanding, but many students have reported that the process of refining the same piece of writing has boosted their confidence. As the script is part of a larger goal, students are also more invested in the writing process. Ana described how the desire to create a quality script prompted her to investigate the past perfect tense in earnest:

> *I have to go to the library, borrow a book to check the tense. I never, never, never do that until this time because was worried about that so it was really good for my English.*
>
> (Ana, Mexico)

Step 6 – Images and storyboarding

When their scripts are reasonably developed, the students then make a storyboard, indicating the kind of pictures they intend to use. This invariably leads to alterations in the script as ideas that can be shown can replace written text thereby achieving more 'economy'. Students are free to use or create their own photographs, or find copyright-free images online. As a lead-in to storyboarding, I often do a drama activity using the convention of tableaux.

Tableaux

While typically a convention for engaging in fictional worlds, tableaux or 'freeze frames' have also been successfully used in the exploration of personal narratives (Hughes & Johnson, 1998). I have used tableaux in two main ways. First, in small groups, the students create a freeze frame of a scene from the beginning, middle and end, after listening to one member's story. In some cases, the author also gives directions to the group and helps sculpt the piece. This is repeated for each group member and then the sculptures are presented to the rest of the class for questioning. An alternative which takes less time is to have the students make frozen statues of the beginning, middle and end of their own stories and discuss these in pairs or small groups.

Some students have reported that this activity helped them express their feelings and it generated ideas for their storyboards.

> *It was good as i thought about the point i emphasis on in my story.*
> *also, it helped me think that what string of picture i choose to deliver my feelings.*
>
> (Chan, Korea)

> *Freeze frame activities made my draft's image more elaborate and made me empathized. I could look myself and think more deeply. Moreover, it gave me another idea, so I could add it into my draft.*
>
> (Sun Young, Korea)

As noted earlier in this chapter, digital stories are multimodal texts, the creation of which has the potential to build multimodal communicative competence (Royce, 2002). To introduce students to the basics of visual grammar (Kress & van Leeuwen, 1996) and the use of metaphor, we often read and analyse a children's picture book called *Piggybook* by Anthony Browne (1996). This is something I often call in the 'experts' for, which leads to another short enactment activity.

Back in role as a conference organiser, I ask the film makers a favour:

Well everyone, this has been an amazing conference, hasn't it? We still have this afternoon's exciting programme ahead, but before that I have another favour to ask you. This one comes from a friend of mine who is a kindergarten teacher. You see, there is a new part of the curriculum that they need to teach called visual literacy. Usually literacy means ability to read and write – but in this multimedia age a lot of communication is done via images. My friend and her colleagues have been asked to use this book [show them Piggybook] and desperately want your advice about how to interpret the images. As film makers, you make these kind of decisions everyday – the choice of camera angles – what to highlight – what to leave out – what that means for the story. Can you help them?

Step 7 – Voice-overs

Before recording their final voice-overs, the students record audio drafts of their story using the free open-source software program Audacity. For many students, it is the first time they have recorded their voices and it raises their awareness about their weaknesses and strengths. Having to record their voices as part of a digital story project also gives students a pretext for practising their pronunciation, with many of them listening repeatedly to my audio feedback and re-recording their voices several times.

In addition to individual feedback, the audio drafts also form the basis of some all-class pronunciation activities which involve elements of drama. These usually begin with vocal warm-ups (see Poston-Anderson's *Drama: Learning Connections in Primary Schools* (2008, pp. 171–179) for a great list of activities exploring vocal expression). Phonemes and words that are problematic across the group are then practised in the form of a rap. For example, the following verse is designed to target sounds that many of my students have problems with: $/\theta/$ and $/ɜ:/$

Pronunciation rap

I'm so thirsty CLAP
So thirsty, oh yeah, CLAP, CLAP
So thirsty, so thirsty, so thirsty.

In role again as the conference organiser, I explain that one year has passed since the last conference. They are back in town for the International Film Festival and about to attend the opening-night party.

Pronunciation role-play dialogue

I give each film maker a card with a movie title, genre and one-sentence plot summary for their 'must-see' movie at the festival, which again targets their particular pronunciation needs. Time permitting, another idea would be to have the students write their own 'scripts' incorporating the words they need to practise. After a few minutes to rehearse their summary, I then distribute name tags. The names also feature the problem phonemes /θ/ and ɜ/ː/, e.g. Ethan, Bertha, Jonathon, Samantha, Thurston. Name tags on, I demonstrate the dialogue with one student and then the role-play begins with the film makers mingling and talking to each other. Party music plays in the background.

Example role-play dialogue:

A: Oh hi.... [*B's name*] How great to see you here.

B: Oh hi there [*A's name*] Good to see you too – it's been ages.

A: I know. Hey, I'm really excited about this year's festival – there are so many great films.

A: I know what you mean. Have you decided which ones you want to see?

B: Well, I've taken a quick look at the program, and one movie that really stands out for me is: Title: *[put the title of your movie here]* It's about ... *[give plot summary here]*

A: Sounds *[insert adjective]*. When it is on?

B: Thursday at 6.30 in the Universal Theatre in the city. What about you, what's your pick for the festival?

A: Well, you know I love a good *[choose a genre, e.g. thriller, rom com, blockbuster, action movie etc]* so I'm keen to see: *[insert title and plot]*. It's on Thursday at 11.30 in the Woolston Cinema.

B: Hmmm, that does sound [adjective] ... [looking away] Oh... look there's C _____ [name of another film maker] over there. Excuse me, *[A]* but I must go and say hello to her/him. It was great to see you again [*A's name*]. Catch you later around the festival

A: Sure, it was good to see you too, [*B's name*].

Step 8 – Music

As with images, I direct students towards copyright-free music. Resources permitting, students can make their own music as well. This step is usually left until towards the end as music can be omitted if there are time constraints.

Step 9 – Putting it all together

Digital stories are compiled using free movie-making software: Movie Maker 2 for windows and iMovie for Apple MacIntosh computers. Before finalising the movies, we have a rough cut viewing of each student's work. This is an opportunity to get valuable feedback on whether the story is communicating the desired message, whether the images are congruent, and whether the volume of the voice and music is adequately balanced.

Step 10 – Final viewing

The final screening, be it for an intimate or larger audience, is a vital step in the process. Students invest incredible amounts of time and effort in making their digital stories. The final screening honours this effort, and honours them. It is a truly moving experience and students are left with a genuine sense of achievement.

Conclusion

After my first digital storytelling project one of my colleagues said enthusiastically, 'This is what teaching can be.' Both digital storytelling and drama in the language classroom go beyond the development of language skills. They are ways for students to engage their creativity, express their identities, learn about self and other, and find their voices. For me, they have made for the most satisfying moments in my teaching career and I encourage readers of this chapter to try them for themselves.

References

Abbs, P. (1989). *A is for aesthetic: Essays on creative and aesthetic education*. New York: Falmer Press.

Arnold. (2005). *Empathic intelligence*. Sydney: University of New South Wales Press.

Banaszewski, T. (2005). Digital storytelling: Supporting digital literacy in Grades 4–12. Unpublished Masters Thesis, Georgia Institute of Technology, Atlanta.

Browne, A. (1996). *Piggybook*. London: Walker Books.

Bruner, J. (1994). Life as narrative. In A. H. Dyson, & C. Genishi (Eds.), *The need for story: Cultural diversity in classroom and community* (pp. 28–37). Urbana, IL: National Council of Teachers of English.

Carter, R. (2007). Response to special issue of *Applied Linguistics* devoted to language creativity in everyday contexts. *Applied Linguistics, 28*(4), 597–608.

CDS (date unspecified). Center for Digital Storytelling. Retrieved 18/04/2011, from www.storycenter.org/principles.html

Cummins, J. (2006). Identity texts: The imaginative construction of self through multiliteracies pedagogy. In O. Garcia, T. Skutkabb-Kangas, & M. Torres-Guzman (Eds.), *Imagining multilingual schools* (pp. 51–68). Buffalo, OH: Multilingual Matters.

Dörnyei, Z., & Malderez, A. (1997). Group dynamics and foreign language teaching. *System, 25*(1), 65–81.

Dörnyei, Z., & Murphey, T. (2003). *Group dynamics in the language classroom*. Cambridge: Cambridge University Press.

Ellis, R. (2003). *Task-based language learning and teaching*. Oxford: Oxford University Press.

Ewing, R., & Simons, J. (2004). *Beyond the script: Drama in the classroom*. Newton, Sydney: PETA.

Fleming, M. (2006). Justifying the arts: Drama and intercultural education [Electronic Version]. *The Journal of Aesthetic Education, 40*, 54–64. Retrieved 18/04/2011 from http://muse.uq.edu.au.ezproxy1.library.usyd.edu.au/journals/the_journal_of_aesthetic_education/v040/40.1fleming.html

Heathcote, D., & Bolton, G. (1994). *Drama for learning: Dorothy Heathcote's mantle of the expert approach to education*. Portsmouth: Heinemann.

Hughes, J. (1993). Linguistic and cultural barriers: The role of drama. In W. Michaels (Ed.), *Drama in education: The state of the art II* (pp. 130–123). Sydney: Educational Drama Association.

Hughes, J., & Arnold, R. (2008). Drama and the teaching of poetry. In M. Anderson, J. Hughes, & J. Manuel (Eds.), *Drama and English teaching: Imagination, action and engagement* (pp. 88–103). South Melbourne: Oxford University Press.

Hughes, J., & Johnson, D. (1998). Drama from intra-subjective monologues and narratives of self. In J. Saxton, & C. Miller (Eds.), *Drama and theatre in education* (pp. 21–30).Victoria, BC: IDEA Publications.

Kress, G., & van Leeuwen, T. (1996). *Reading images: The grammar of visual design*. New York: Routledge.

Lambert, J. (2002). *Digital storytelling: Capturing lives, creating community*. Berkeley, CA: Digital Diner Press.

Liu, J. (2002). Process drama in second and foreign-language classrooms. In G. Brauer (Ed.), *Body and language: Intercultural learning through drama* (pp. 51–70). London: Ablex Publishing.

Marschke, R. (2005). Creating contexts, characters, and communication: Foreign language teaching and process drama. Unpublished Masters Thesis, QUT.

McGeoch, K., & Hughes, J. (2009). Digital storytelling and drama. In M. Anderson, J. Carroll, & D. Cameron (Eds.), *Drama education and digital technology*. London: Continuum.

Morgan, N., & Saxton, J. (1987). *Teaching drama: A mind of many wonders*. London: Hutchinson.

Neelands, J. (1990). *Structuring drama work*. Cambridge: Cambridge University Press.

Nelson, M. (2006). Mode, meaning, and synaesthesia in multimedia L2 writing. [Electronic Version]. *Language Learning & Technology, 10*, 56–76. Retrieved 18/04/2011 from http://llt.msu.edu/vol-10num2/pdf/nelson.pdf

New London Group. (2000). A pedadgogy of multiliteracies: Designing social futures. In B. Cope, & M. Kalantzis (Eds), *Multiliteracies: Literacy learning and the design of social futures*. Melbourne: Macmillan.

Norton, B. (2010). Language and identity. In N. Hornberger, & S. McKay (Eds.), *Sociolinguistics and language education* (pp. 349–369). Clevedon, UK: Multilingual Matters.

Ohler, J. (2008). *Digital storytelling in the classroom*. Thousand Oaks, CA: Corwin Press.

Poston-Anderson, B. (2008). *Drama: Learning connections in primary schools*. Melbourne: Oxford University Press.

Royce, T. D. (2002). *Multimodality in the TESOL classroom: Exploring visual–Verbal synergy* (Vol. 36, pp. 191–205): Teachers of English to Speakers of Other Languages, Inc. (TESOL).

Scarino, A., & Liddicoat, A. J. (2009). *Teaching and learning languages: A guide*. Australian Government: Department of Education, Employment and Workplace Relations.

Senior, R. (2002). A class-centred approach to language teaching. *ELT Journal, 56*(4), 397–403.

Van Lier, L. (1996). *Interaction in the language curriculum: Awareness, autonomy & authenticity*. New York: Longman.

Van Lier, L. (1998). The relationship between consciousness, interaction and language learning. *Language Awareness, 7*(2&3), 128–145.

Van Lier, L. (2004). *The ecology and semiotics of language learning: A sociocultural perspective*. Boston: Kluwer Academic.

Van Lier, L. (2007). From communicative competence to semiotic competence. In E. Werlen, & R. Weskamp (Eds.), *Kommunikakative Kompetenz and Mehrsprachigkeit* (pp. 49–58). Esslingen, Germany: Schneider Verlag Hohengehren GmbH.

Wolfe, S., & Alexander, R. (2008). *Argumentation and dialogic teaching: Alternative pedagogies for a changing world*. Retrieved 18/04/2011, from www.robinalexander.org.uk/docs/wolfealexander.pdf

Film and Drama Aesthetics for Additional Language Teaching[*]

Erika C. Piazzoli

In this chapter I outline how combining dramatic and filmic modes can offer Additional Language learners an experiential insight into the target language. For this purpose, I designed a sequence of drama workshops based on the narrative of a short film, working to build a shared aesthetic and to promote communicative, intercultural and affective engagement.

As the short film selected is a silent piece, the strategies outlined below can be adapted to suit any Additional Language (AL) classroom. In my specific context, the 15-hour process drama was conducted with a group of intermediate Italian (AL) speakers. This course was structured as a five-day intensive, but it could be easily adapted into a secondary school term schedule.

The work draws from a case study designed for my doctoral research on the aesthetics of process drama for AL teaching. In this chapter I will focus on praxis – applying theory to classroom practice, while touching briefly on the pragmatics of the research. In particular, my aim here is to map out practical strategies that integrate film and process drama aesthetics together with AL teaching methodologies.

Process drama for Additional Language learning

My educational focus in using drama pedagogy in the AL classroom is centred upon spontaneous communication in the target language. After ten years of practice, I believe that my challenge as an AL teacher remains to create the conditions for *spontaneous* communication in the classroom. In effect, I found that often, as an AL teacher, I deal with *artificial* communication, where speakers interact according to set classroom dynamics unique to the classroom environment.

[*]Author's note: in this chapter Additional Language (AL) is used as an umbrella term to include Second Language.

I believe that process drama is a useful approach to create the conditions for spontaneous communication. It is grounded in the notion of 'play', which Bruner (1983) conceptualised as a safe vehicle for trying out combinations of behaviours without pressure, minimising the consequences on one's actions thanks to the fictional dimension. Although initially directed at children, process drama considers 'play' as a highly developed form of cognitive activity and it has been widely transposed to adult learning (O'Toole, 1992). Its foundations are built on constructivist theories of learning, according to which knowledge is not passively poured into students' heads, but constructed by each learner (Wagner, 1998).

Process drama also resonates with psychodynamic pedagogy, according to which an effective pedagogy engages thinking and feeling at inter-personal and intra-personal levels. In this sense, it has been argued that it is a cornerstone of psychodynamic pedagogy, as it has the potential to enhance affective awareness through projection and identification in a role (Arnold 1994, p. 21). It develops empathic intelligence and is rooted in the belief that the most effective learning occurs when cognition and affect are engaged in the service of learning (Hughes & Arnold, 2008).

The intrinsic qualities of process drama can be beneficial to AL learning as they engage the body and the mind, not only to produce language, but also to express emotions and ideas through gesture, posture and facial expression, the bases of non-verbal communication. As a result, it helps to make direct connections between visual/kinaesthetic stimuli and AL oral production, facilitating creative thinking in the target language.

Process drama can also stimulate engagement with the language. Van Lier (1996) defines Additional Language engagement in terms of how *receptive* the learner is to the language to which they are exposed. He visualises this engagement as a continuum, from 'being unaware', to 'being vigilant' of the language:

+ + + being unaware   being vigilant – – –

Van Lier explains AL engagement in terms of creating *curiosity* or *receptivity* in the AL speaker. Drawing from Allwright and Bailey (1991), he defines receptivity as 'a state of mind, whether permanent or temporary, that is open to the experience of becoming a speaker of another language' (Van Lier, 1996, p 48). This 'receptivity' undoubtedly needs to stem from the speaker's intrinsic motivation, which will vary according to the individual. But how can an AL teacher encourage this state of mind?

Van Lier argues that AL learning occurs *between* lessons, not *during* lessons (1996, p. 43). In other words, the lesson needs to stimulate the learner to create empathy with the content material and to think about it beyond the class.

This concept aligns well with O'Neill's description of process drama, in terms of an aesthetic experience that offers an alternative way of seeing ourselves (1995, p. 152). It also echoes Bundy's definition of aesthetic engagement, in terms of developing a heightened awareness as a result of the engagement in a dramatic experience. Such heightened awareness, I believe, can make the AL speaker become more receptive to the target language; this was my intention in designing and facilitating the structure outlined below.

Process drama for AL learning

The AL teacher interested in a process drama approach needs to be familiar with the concept of *pre-text*, the initial stimulus that triggers the dramatic action. This can be a story, a photograph, a film, a poem, a newspaper article or any item that can provide the initial motivation and curiosity to explore a dramatic context. The pre-text, as O'Neill (1995, p. 43) argues, needs to be dramatic enough to 'bind the group together in anticipation; in a good pre-text, dramatic tension will already be implied, roles suggested, and action anticipated.'

Defined by Kao and O'Neill as 'mental excitement' (1998), dramatic tension is one of the fundamental elements of drama. In particular, tension is an essential device of the art form, which directly influences the level of engagement in the drama. As O'Toole and Dunn remark, the greater the challenge for the participants, the greater the tension, the deeper and more lasting the learning experience (2002, p. 21).

When it comes to AL process drama, the issue of tension implied in the pre-text becomes even more delicate, because it is the teacher's responsibility to ensure it has a dramatic potential without creating a language barrier. For this reason, when working with AL students, there are advantages in selecting a pre-text that is graphic in nature. Using illustrations, photographs, animations or film, the AL teacher can rely on a stimulus that communicates a situation visually.

Film as pre-text

The film I selected is the multi-award winning *Buongiorno* (2005), written and directed by Melo Prino and produced by BêkaFilms. A five-minute silent piece, the film creates a grotesque mood and features a strong aesthetic component, both in terms of filmic and dramatic elements.

The narrative structure of the film revolves around the morning ritual of brushing teeth in front of the mirror. By manipulating elements such as sound, rhythm, repetition and editing, the film manages to create a strong aesthetic from the very basic idea of waking up in the morning. A middle aged man (below) wakes up, goes to the bathroom and brushes his teeth in front of the mirror, to find his reflection mocking him. This sequence is repeated several times in a dramatic crescendo.

There is only one word uttered in the whole film: '*buongiorno!*' (good morning!) which the reflection shouts at the protagonist. For the rest of the film, there is no dialogue but an epic-western soundtrack (composed by Ennio Morricone), a motif which plays a pivotal role in differentiating between being awake and asleep. The mood created by the soundtrack evokes a duel, with the protagonist succumbing to his own delusions in the mirror.

All participants in my group came from extremely different cultural and socio-economic contexts. However, regardless of experience, they were all studying Italian as an Additional Language. As this was their main shared experience, I decided to design a drama based on this context and imagined that the protagonist of the film was in fact a *teacher of Italian*.

FIGURE 11.1 Scene from the film *Buongiorno*

The drama I created explores *what* could have happened to the protagonist afterwards. I imagined that he experienced a shock and thereafter refused to speak, his last words being 'today/I am/not/very communicative'. He had since then fallen into a trance-like state, and it was up to the students, enrolled as psychologists, to help him emerge from his crisis and start talking again.

As will be evident, the situation I set up is quite ironic: whereas conventionally it is the teacher whose aim is to help students communicate, this drama begins with the roles completely reversed – the AL teacher unable to speak, with the students in role as expert psychologists to help him.

Film and drama aesthetics

In the process drama structure below I relied on my understanding of film and drama aesthetics to create the conditions for spontaneous communication in the target language. Understanding and combining the *elements of drama*, as listed by Haseman and O'Toole (2000) and the *elements of film*, as defined by Bordwell and Thompson (1997), the teacher can develop strategies to enhance AL learning.

Elements of film:

- Setting
- Lighting
- Costume
- Movement

- Focus & depth of field
- Framing
- Editing
- Sound.

Elements of drama:

- Role & situation
- Tension
- Focus
- Symbol
- Language & movement
- Place & space
- Mood
- Meaning.

At this stage, it must be remembered that the AL classroom is *not* a film- or drama-specialised class; its main purpose is for students to learn a foreign language. Thus, students do not need to analyse drama or film form; it is the teacher who needs to be aware of it

FIGURE 11.2 Scene from the film *Buongiorno*

and help the students to recognise it. The film and drama elements can help the teacher to structure a lesson, so that students can creatively engage with the target language through visual, auditory and kinaesthetic modes of learning.

For example, the photograph above (the final revenge of the reflections) can be used as a platform for discussion in terms of several aspects: its content (using descriptive language), its filmic composition (discussing film aesthetics) and its implications (exploring dramatic elements). By describing the elements in the frame, and then voicing the thoughts of the different reflections in the mirror, participants can effectively combine film aesthetics with drama strategies to fuel their creativity in the target language.

The structure

In creating this structure I have drawn on O'Toole and Dunn's (2002) template for designing process dramas. This includes three phases: initiation, experience and reflection. The initiation phase is where a shared belief in roles and situations is negotiated with the students. This concept, Owens and Barber have argued, is essential to the success of the drama (2005). The experiential phase is where students experience the interweaving of process drama conventions, while the reflective phase is where they process their experiences to make meaning from them (O'Toole & Dunn, 2002, p. 24).

The first step when beginning a drama workshop is to reach mutual agreement from the participants to commit to the work. The 'drama contract' gives individuals ownership of their drama. As Owens and Barbers (2005, p. 7) put it: 'if [participants] do not believe that the drama belongs to them, then the scope for learning is reduced'. After obtaining mutual agreement to begin the drama, the teacher can follow the basic structure below, keeping in mind that each drama will be different based on the input of the participants.

This structure can be divided into a sequence of seven two-hour workshops, or 15 one-hour sessions, according to the specific educational contexts. It is a flexible structure which can be re-arranged by the teacher according to the creative input and the needs of the group.

Initiation phase

STRATEGY	COMMENT
Launching the pre-text. Watch the short film Buongiorno (2005). www.bekafilms.it/html/showreel_ buongiorno.html (used with the permission of BêkaFilms)	This is a visual pre-text which can work well in an AL context as it creates dramatic tension through images and sound.
Discussion. Discuss the mood of the film. What effect does it create on the viewer? Why? Comment and watch the film again.	Students can suggest a series of keywords (emotions / sensations / free association) for the teacher to write on the board.

(Continued)

(Continued)

STRATEGY	COMMENT
Language warm up.	
Pick a partner and describe in detail the content of the film.	AL speakers are translating the visual stimuli directly into the target language.
Drama warm up.	
Watch the film again. Working with the same partner, create three open questions for the group. After five minutes share the questions and let the group answer.	Here we start to question the pre-text and consider the possibilities it offers for dramatic action, stimulating a state of curiosity.
Dramatic re-interpretation of the film.	
In pairs, create a) A voiceover describing the film in third person. b) A line/ some dialogue for each reflection, in first person. After 15–20 minutes ask each pair to present a section, by narrating their piece alongside the film.	It is important that the AL teacher assists students in this task. By giving language feedback, the students will feel more confident once they present to the group.
Dramatic contract.	
Inform the group that, from now on, we will use this film as a platform into a fictional world. We will imagine that this man works as an AL teacher in a nearby school (let students decide which one or invent one). Let the participants choose a name, a title and an age for the man. From now on, refer to him by his last name.	To help the AL speaker visualise the idea, write on the board the chosen name, his age and his profession, next to a sketch of his face:  Name: Mr ____ Age: _____ AL teacher
Role on the wall.	
Draw on the board a silhouette of the man and ask learners to define this role more in-depth. Write the physical traits outside, the emotional traits inside the silhouette.	This activity is useful to review language related to body parts and personality traits. 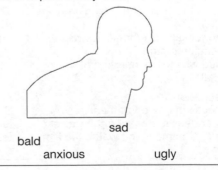 sad bald anxious ugly

STRATEGY	COMMENT
Teacher narration. Use all the details on the board to create a narration of the man's routine. An example: … as we know, [X] works as an AL teacher. Usually he is always on time for class. Yesterday, however, his students waited for him … they waited, waited and waited. It was cold outside. He never arrived. Why? The secretary tried to call him, but his mobile phone was disconnected. At home, the answering machine was on; the message was a bit strange …	Here the AL teacher becomes a storyteller; it is essential for the teacher to narrate the story using expressive, sensory language. The teacher may guide the group into a short breathing/relaxation exercise before the narration starts and ask them to listen to the narration with eyes closed. After the listening task, a language recap will be necessary to make sure the content has been understood by all.
Creating the answering machine message. In small groups, create the man's answering machine message. Write a short script and use the voice to interpret it. After 10–15 minutes, present to the rest of the class.	Interpreting the text through voice may include playing with keywords, pace, pauses, repetition, echo and so on. The teacher can assist each group both with the pronunciation and interpretation.
Teacher narration. Pick up from the previous narration to continue the story, adding that [X] has been reported missing to the Police. He was eventually found, in quite delicate circumstances … A team of psychologists has been called to intervene.	The teacher functions as an omniscient narrator, providing more clues to the story. Focusing on the expressivity of the story will add dramatic tension to the drama, which in turn will fuel motivation to speak.
Mantle of the Expert. Inform the students that, for the purpose of this drama, we will all become members of the team of psychologists and will try to help [X] recover from his crisis and to talk again.	'Mantle of the Expert' entails enrolling the students as 'experts' in the fictional context. It is very effective as it flips the teacher/student status relationship (see Heathcote & Bolton, 1995).
Hand out role cards for names, age, expertise (already provided for each participant) personality and hobby. As an example, re-create the same form on the board and complete together. Allow a few minutes for each to create their role.	Example: NAME: Dr_____ COGNITIVE PSYCHOLOGIST AGE: _____ PERSONALITY:_____ HOBBY: _____

(Continued)

(Continued)

STRATEGY	COMMENT
Hot seat. In groups of three, the psychologists interview each other to develop their roles (five mins each). Two participants (out of role) ask questions to the person in the hot seat (in role).	Working in small groups helps the AL speaker feel safe in the improvisation. At this stage, the teacher is stimulating that state of receptivity which Van Lier (1996) identifies as necessary to language learning.
Sharing the roles. Everyone introduces his/her role in a circle by providing the information scaffolded on the role card, as well as some details to have emerged during the hot seat. The teacher also introduces his/her role as psychologist and as team coordinator (teacher in role).	Here we begin to see how process drama relies on a constructivist approach to develop learning: the participants have created their own roles and are beginning to interact in the target language using their own resources.

Experiential phase

STRATEGY	COMMENT
Teacher in role. Position the chairs to suggest a meeting. The teacher makes use of a prop (glasses, hat etc.), takes on his/her role as the coordinator and addresses the team. This is an example: Dear colleagues, thank you for coming to this emergency meeting. As you all know, our main concern at the moment is for our annual conference to run smoothly; if it does, research funds will be allocated to the team for next year. There is however a small problem ... [alarmed] we don't have a case to present yet! Remember that call from the police last Monday? It is not a very glamorous case, but ... it's the only one we have, so we'll have to use it for our presentation. [Whispering] of course, none of the delegates is to suspect this. Our reputation needs to remain high, as it is tied to the annual research funds that will be allocated at the end of the conference ...	For the AL teacher, 'teacher in role' is an invaluable tool as it exposes the learners to alternative registers of language, which the teacher would not be able to model otherwise (Kao & O'Neill, 1998). When engaged in 'teacher in role', the AL teacher needs to speak with a suitable register and pace, trying to minimise the 'teacher talk' which usually characterises his/her language (talking at a slower pace, using simplified language, emphasising gestures etc.). Immediately after the 'teacher in role' episode, the AL teacher needs to allow time for a post-episode reflection, during which the teacher goes back into his/her natural role and helps the learners to unpack the language used, in order to process its content. Colloquial, idiomatic expressions used by the teacher in role can then be pointed out.

STRATEGY	COMMENT

Setting the situation. Still in role, present the clinical case: the subject [X] was apparently a healthy man, employed as a teacher in a nearby language school. He was found in a trance-like state inside the lift of his own apartment block. His last words were: 'today I am not very communicative'. He refuses to leave the lift. He has stopped talking. The teams will need to develop an action plan. Any questions? The coordinator will be back in [30 minutes] to discuss their action plans and formulate a strategy to intervene on the subject.

Writing the action plans.

In small groups, the psychologists can discuss possible intervention strategies. They need to create an action plan to remove the man from the lift and take him to the hospital without any further traumas. Leave 15–20 minutes for discussion and writing, then share the action plans.

Possible examples:

- Tell the man we are here to help
- Offer him food / water
- Cover the mirrors in the lift

The instructions for this task have been given by the 'teacher in role'; it is therefore essential for the teacher to recapitulate them out of role, answering questions and doing examples on the board.

During the writing phase, the AL teacher needs to offer ongoing language support and feedback so that, when they are ready to present in role, the AL speakers feel confident enough to present a written document which is grammatically and lexically sound.

Individual role plays.

Set up different role plays, according to what emerged in the improvisations. Some possibilities could be: a role play between the psychologist and the man's neighbour, his colleagues, his students and/or the school director. After the role plays, get all the participants who were in role as psychologists to report back to the team.

This is the first real opportunity in the workshop for the AL learners to engage in a meaningful role play in the target language. The pressure of improvising in a foreign language should be minimised by the fact that the focus is on content, rather than form, and that the role plays are occurring simultaneously in the space.

Informal report.

At the end of the role play, summarise the outcome of the interviews in an informal report, to be shared by the team. The coordinator (teacher in role) asks the team to draw further conclusions about the man's possible state.

This episode is useful for the AL speaker as it essentially re-elaborates and processes the language into a different context (from formal interview with a higher status to informal report with equal status). This can lead to reflection on register and language variation.

(Continued)

STRATEGY	COMMENT

Tableaux.

In groups of four–five, participants choose one option from the action plan and represent the outcome of the strategy through a freeze frame. Allow five minutes for brainstorming, ten to organise the tableaux.

For this activity to be successful in the AL class, it is imperative that the learners commit to using the target language during the negotiation. If necessary, the teacher can review body parts and imperative tenses to provide the right scaffolding for this task.

When presenting one group at a time, get the other groups to observe and guess the idea behind the work.

Teacher narration.

Build from the students' ideas to narrate the outcome of the action plans. Add that unfortunately shortly after their visit, [X]'s state has degenerated into violence and he has been hospitalised. They will need to inform his family.

This teacher narration serves the purpose of injecting dramatic tension and advancing the narrative. It also provides a link to the next written activity.

Letters to the family.

Let the group decide what family members to contact. Get participants to choose one family member and write a formal letter to inform them of the situation and summon them to a (confidential) interview.

Once again, by letting the group decide which family members are relevant to the story, the teacher is delegating the creative power to students as co-artists. This is a source of motivation to the learners who are active creators of the fictional context.

Allow 10–15 minutes for writing the letters. Ask a few volunteers to read them out and collect the others for language feedback and/or assessment purposes.

If necessary, a review on how to write formal letters will be needed. As above, some AL feedback/ support can be given at the time of drafting, to ensure that students feel more confident to present their work in front of the group.

Intercultural discussion.

How is mental health seen by the society of the country you come from? Is it a taboo or is it openly discussed among family units? What about in [target culture]? Engage the group in a discussion in small groups and then together.

Depending upon the age and maturity of the teaching group, such moments of discussion are of the highest value for the depth of the AL drama experience. The AL teacher needs continuously to be tuned to possible hooks for intercultural reflection and openly challenge the group to contribute to them.

The letter.

The team coordinator shows a letter from [X] addressed to the psychologists. The letter warns them not to contact his family as they do not have to know his mental state.

The letter is a source of tension as it reveals the man's motivation (not to disclose his health state to his family) against the facts (his family has already been contacted).

Hand out one copy each and allow time for individual reading, language comprehension and discussion on the tone of the letter.

It also functions as an experiential hook to the intercultural dimension which was discussed in the previous episode.

STRATEGY	COMMENT
Group role play.	
Let the group choose three family members that they want to interview. The whole team will interview one person at a time. Draft interview questions before starting.	It is important to encourage the AL learners to draft the questions, in order to scaffold appropriate language which will be later used in the improvisation.
Give separate instructions to the three family members: they refuse to accept this situation, for them mental health is taboo. They need to protect the image of the family and pretend everything is fine.	By giving the interviewees a different rationale, the teacher sets up conflicting agendas in the interviews: this increases the dramatic tension, once again shifting the linguistic focus from form to content.
Writing an interview report.	
Write a short, detailed report of the interview and present it to the rest of the team.	Provide the necessary structural support: first write the facts (as they emerged from the interview) then the interpretation.
Interviewing the man.	
The coordinator has read the reports and is very pleased, as the case has turned out to be very interesting and the team will be able to present it at the conference. Now what is left is to interview the subject. Discuss and decide the best strategy to tackle him (where to interview him, what questions to ask etc.).	At this stage, it is likely that the AL speakers have engaged with the target language, developing that 'vigilant state of curiosity' (Van Lier, 1996) necessary to sustain an improvisation with a degree of spontaneity.
The escape.	
The 'teacher in role' leaves to escort the subject to the interview. He/she returns in an alarmed state, holding his pyjamas. [X] is missing! He has escaped from the ward!	In this episode the dramatic tension is at its highest. Allow the group to improvise for as long as the tension remains high.
Gossip mill.	
Instruct the group to move around the space. They need to imagine they are in the hospital, five minutes after they've learned about the escape. Use the soundtrack from the film as a signal to start/stop moving: as the music stops, students form pairs and begin to gossip about the subject's whereabouts. Repeat three or four times.	Before starting the 'gossip mill' model an example of a possible interaction and provide a language structure which they can use to begin, such as: 'have you heard that ...' Using the soundtrack of the film re-creates its mood and gives rhythm to the drama.
Tableaux vivant.	
In small groups, brainstorm ideas about the whereabouts of [X] and represent one possibility through a tableau vivant. Allow time to discuss and decide a possible development for the story. After 15–20 minutes, present it to the class.	A 'tableau vivant' is similar to a freeze frame but includes movement and language. Approach the exercise to support not only the students' language, but also their dramatic representations.

(Continued)

(Continued)

STRATEGY	COMMENT
Teacher narration.	
Narrate the continuation of the story, incorporating the plot of the tableaux vivant into the narration. Conclude that [X] has been found alive.	The teacher needs to have actively attended to the ideas behind the tableaux in order to integrate them into the narration and provide a link with the next narrative step.
Final role play.	
One participant volunteers to take the role of [X], wearing the pyjamas as a symbol. He/she is interviewed by the psychologists.	This is the climax of the drama: participants are likely to have developed a highly affective and intercultural engagement.
Writing the final report.	
Participants can draft a comprehensive report of the case.	The report needs to be checked for AL feedback/ support. Alternatively it can be collected for assessment.
Whole class drama.	
Set up the space to simulate a conference room. The coordinator welcomes the delegates and introduces the case study, asking the psychologists to present the case. After all have been heard, the coordinator thanks them and closes the conference.	This episode concludes the experiential phase of the drama. The students should have had enough AL support to feel confident in reading out their reports to an (imaginary) audience, once again strengthening the vocabulary learned in class.

Reflective phase

After each workshop, it is important to allow enough time for reflection. In the AL process drama workshop, reflection can be of a dramatic, intercultural and linguistic nature:

- ■ 'Dramatic reflection' refers to de-briefing activities, such as pair or group discussion. Reflection can be done in role (through writing and/or speaking out the thoughts of the characters, either collectively or individually) or out of role (through discussion and analysis).

- ■ 'Intercultural reflection' refers to activities intended to expose the different cultural perceptions that have emerged during the workshops. It can be done at the end of each workshop as a debate, between episodes and at any stage of the drama. It is up to the AL teacher to sense what themes are emerging and invite participants to reflect upon them.

- ■ 'Linguistic reflection' refers to a comprehensive summary of all language items to have emerged during the drama. From here, the AL teacher can link to the introduction and/or review of particular grammar structures, semantic areas and idiomatic expressions. It is the AL teacher's responsibility to be aware of the new expressions and to find the means for students to remember them at the end of each class.

Managing the drama

The drama outlined above can be divided into a sequence of five three-hour workshops, seven two-hour workshops or fifteen one-hour sessions, according to particular contexts. Regardless, it is important to balance each session, making sure it contains a proper *initiation* phase (where the pre-text is resumed, by watching it, re-creating it etc), a substantial *experiential* phase and a comprehensive *reflection* phase.

As already discussed, AL learning occurs *between* lessons, not *during* lessons (Van Lier, 1996). To provide links between sessions that re-focus the group, the teacher needs to manage the drama structure properly. This can be done by offering language, film and drama activities at the beginning and/or at the end of the workshops, in order to reconnect with the story and reinforce the learning.

■ *Language-orientated* activities will vary in complexity according to the group proficiency. They are useful to resume/recap the language that emerged in the workshop. In order to design these, the AL teacher needs to keep a written record of the new expressions as they emerge. They can include guessing games (drawing/miming new expressions), matching drawings with definitions, finding the synonym, group competitions or others, drawing from an AL teaching repertoire.

■ As for *drama-orientated* strategies, their purpose will be to focus and create group cohesion. Drawing from the drama teacher's repertoire, many games can be used to link sessions and create empathy. In this particular drama, the classic 'mirror exercise' is ideal as it echoes the main concept of the film. The mirroring game (two people in front of each other, one mirroring the other) can be proposed with the variations of the reflections becoming animated and progressively defiant.

■ *Film-orientated* activities include discussing the elements of film and what effects they have on the viewer. Students can identify the repetitive structure of the film, discuss the role of editing, lighting and framing, as well as working with the soundtrack (from understanding its role and the mood it creates to free association, free movement etc.). Using the film *without audio* can link sessions; without sound, the students can create the voiceover for the story, dub the different personalities and so on. Conversely, using the audio *without the visuals*, the students can describe the content of the film. Also, using the *storyboard* is another effective tool to get students to reconstruct the narrative, create text and link the film to the drama effectively.

It will be evident that, when managing the AL process drama, the teacher needs to be wearing multiple hats: the *drama teacher hat*, which demands attention to the aesthetic dimension of the class, and the *AL teacher hat*, which focuses on the communicative aspect. In addition, when using a film as a pre-text for the drama, the *filmmaker hat* brings attention to the elements of film and how they can be best integrated with language and drama to provide opportunities for communication.

Conclusion

In this chapter I have considered how to combine film and drama for teaching Additional Languages. I have suggested that using filmic and dramatic elements can create a fruitful platform for fuelling the motivation to communicate in an AL.

I have argued, after Van Lier (1996), that to be fully engaged with the language, AL learners need to reach a state of 'receptivity', in which they are 'vigilant' of the target language not only during the lesson, but also afterwards. This requires the AL teacher to create opportunities for experiential learning and for reflection, which can trigger enough curiosity for the speaker to remain vigilant. Such a state of curiosity, I believe, can be achieved through a process drama approach.

References

Allwright, D. & Bailey, K. (1991). *Focus on the language classroom*. Cambridge: Cambridge University Press.

Arnold, R. (1994). Research issues, psychodynamic pedagogy and drama in education. *NADIE, 18*(2), 15–23.

Bordwell, D., & Thompson, K. (1997). *Film art: An introduction*. New York: McGraw-Hill.

Bruner, J. (1983). *Child's talk: Learning to use language*. New York: W.W. Norton.

Haseman, B., & O'Toole J. (2000). *Dramawise*. Victoria: Heinemann.

Heathcote, D., & Bolton, G. (1995). *Drama for learning: An account of Heathcote's mantle of the expert approaches to education*. Portsmouth, NH: Heinemann.

Hughes, J., & Arnold, R. (2008). Drama and the teaching of poetry. In: Manuel J., Hughes J., Anderson, M., & Arnold, R. (Eds), *Drama and English teaching: Imagination, action and engagement* (p. 102). Oxford: Oxford University Press.

Kao, S. M., & O'Neill, C. (1998). *Words into worlds: Learning a second language through process drama*. London: Ablex Publishing.

O'Neill, C. (1995). *Drama worlds: A framework for process drama*. Portsmouth, NH: Heinemann.

O'Toole, J. (1992). *The process of drama: Negotiating art and meaning*, London: Routledge.

O'Toole, J., & Dunn, J. (2002). *Pretending to learn: Helping children through drama*. French Forest: Longman.

Owens, A., & Barbers, K. (2005). *Mapping Drama*. Melbourne: Phoenix Education.

Prino, M. (2005). *Buongiorno*. Bêkafilms: Milan.

Van Lier, L. (1996). *Interaction in the language curriculum*. London: Longman.

Wagner, B. J. (1998). *Educational drama and language arts*. Portsmouth, NH: Heinemann.

Afterword

Joe Winston

After one year of teaching French I was struggling. I had real doubts about pedagogy and purpose, experiencing a great deal of dissatisfaction with text books and curricula and struggling with the question of how to motivate learners with contrasting levels of interest and academic propensity. Then one evening I had the good fortune to hear Mick Buckby from the University of York, UK, speak about his own philosophy of modern language teaching and how he put this into practice in urban schools with high levels of deprivation that were even further away from France than my own. This turned out to be one of those Eureka moments in my professional career and it had a profound effect on how I was to teach in subsequent years. There were two points that he made that I remember still. The first was that language learning of any kind ought to be about communication first, accuracy second. To illustrate this he spoke of how, on the previous evening, his three year-old son had approached him with a picture in his hand saying 'Daddy, look what I've doned!' 'My response, [he said] wasn't to shout at him and say 'Foolish child! Don't you realise that the past participle of the verb "to do" is irregular and does not require an —ed ending!' No, I was first and foremost delighted to hear him speak to me in a perfectly communicable way, delighted that he wanted to speak to me at all, and delighted, too, that he was beginning to internalise some of the rules of English grammar, even if he had yet to master them completely.' From then on I worked at developing a mindset that was delighted whenever a child was willing and able to communicate successfully in French to me and that delighted in the personal progress individuals made, albeit at different rates.

The second point that I recall Buckby making centred around the specific issue of contextual significance; that the content of a foreign or second language lesson was itself significant and should never solely be about learning a set of language skills, as this in itself would not motivate the majority of students to learn. Kirsty McGeoch has made a similar point in the conclusion of Chapter 10 of this book, identifying the second language classroom as a place where students can engage their creativity, express their identities, learn about self and other, and find their own personal voices. Buckby's own series of textbooks, *Action!* emphasised the context of the country itself – how to find one's way around a town; how to meet people; what to buy and where. It placed the emphasis on establishing purposeful contexts so that the language could come alive for students. The schemes of work described in this volume have all put a similar emphasis on context, albeit from a different perspective. They are all richly imaginative, using stories of all kinds to establish vibrant classroom contexts that are nonetheless no more fictional than those which frame activities in which students ask directions around a foreign town or introduce themselves to a new acquaintance. There have been personal tales but also folk tales, fairy tales, tales of adventure, comic and surreal tales and tales from Shakespeare; all of these have featured in one way or another at the heart of these drama schemes. What has mattered has been the imaginative grip these stories have been able to bring, the playful ways in which they have held the interest of the students and stimulated in them a desire to participate and communicate in the target language.

Perhaps this little book with its examples of excellent practice might offer a Eureka moment for some of its readers, but that is not its primary intention. I emphasised in the introduction that the authors are not advocating drama as any kind of fool-proof panacea, as a set of techniques to be copied and emulated irrespective of any understanding of the principles that underpin them. Rather, the book should be seen as attempting to re-enforce and further establish good practices within the fields of both drama and second language learning with underlying, pedagogic principles that share much in common with those I learned from Buckby. Both place an emphasis on communication, motivation, social relationships and meaningful contexts as fundamental to good pedagogic practice. That the pedagogic practices of drama can be challenging for teachers unused to them there can be no denying but, in coming to grips with drama as a playful but powerful pedagogy, teachers can also, I believe, discover (or re-discover) that other virtue hidden within Buckby's story about his young son, namely a sense of delight. This sense of delight has permeated the chapters of this book and can be found in the stories that have gripped the children, the playfulness of the dramatic strategies used by the teachers, the laughter and excitement they describe in their classrooms and the warmth that characterises the students' own comments. Above all, there is delight on the part of the authors in the students' learning, learning not confined to the target languages themselves, central though this is, but a delight that embraces those broader aspects of learning as evidenced in improved social relationships, more active creative engagement and enhanced feelings of self worth.

Glossary of Drama Conventions

Conscience alley

The class is formed in two lines between which a student in role can walk. She/he may be faced with a difficult decision or be on her/his way to an important event in the drama. As she/he walks down the 'alley' the students she/he approaches utter phrases out loud. Perhaps these are her/his thoughts, perhaps one side take the role of 'good angels', the other 'bad angels'.

Formal meeting

The teacher and the children meet in role, following the conventions of a formal meeting. This could be a meeting of the king's advisers, a meeting of local politicians, a meeting of parents and teachers and so on. By following formal conventions students are encouraged to use a formal register of language.

Freeze frames

Here groups work to create an image of a moment in time from their own bodies. Often it will represent people frozen in the middle of some action, but it might also represent a picture found on a palace wall, for example.

Gossip mill

During a gossip mill the students move freely around the drama space and when they encounter someone they report an event, then pass the information on, thus spreading the gossip.

Hot seating

Someone (either teacher or student) assumes a role and is questioned by a group or perhaps the whole class. The taking of the role may be signalled by sitting in a particular seat (the 'hot seat'), by wearing an item of costume (such as a hat) or by holding a particular prop.

Mantle of the Expert
The class take on roles which have specialist knowledge or expertise needed in the drama, such as detectives, medical workers or child psychologists.

Narrated action
The teacher can use narration to introduce, link or conclude action or he/she can narrate events that the students silently act out. Particularly effective when creating an atmosphere of mystery..

Sculpt/model
A student is the clay, his/her partner is the sculptor who sculpts the 'clay' into a statue representing how a character feels or appears at a particular moment. Contrasting / similar examples can be studied and adjectives / phrases sought to describe what the students can see in them.

Shoulder tap
Usually enacted when the learners are frozen in a frame. A member of the frozen group is tapped and he/she comments on the situation in some way. For example it can take the form of expressing how one felt at the frozen point in time, or creating a sentence describing the event.

Sound collage
Sounds are made, often by the whole class using voice, body and/or instruments, either to accompany actions or to create atmosphere.

Teacher in role
The teacher takes on a role and joins in the drama fully. Her/his roles can have a variety of statuses. This is a key strategy for unsettling the normal power relations in the classroom and allows the teacher and the children to engage in forms of questioning and answering with the kind of emotional edge that ordinary teacher–pupil discussion cannot manage.

Thought tracking (or voices in the head)
Students, perhaps in a frozen image, are touched gently on the shoulder and asked to voice the private thoughts or feelings of their character at a particular moment in the drama.

The whoosh (or story wand)
Holding a 'wand' of some kind the teacher narrates a story that the children, sitting in a circle, act out voluntarily. The teacher needs to use many action verbs and adverbs in the narration and should be responsive to the students' own contributions. The actors in the circle are changed at regular intervals when the teacher waves the wand through the air and calls out 'whoosh'!

Index